000002187096

Walkthrough

Read this first - or turn the page to go straight to the story!

The Characters

The Helix

Three teenagers who can turn into animals.

Mato

Mato is one of the Helix. He is a good leader. He can change into a bear.

Kes

Kes is one of the Helix. She is funny and a good learner. She can change into a kestrel.

Shak

Shak is one of the Helix. He is shy but good at sneaking. He can change into a snake.

Key Facts

The Tainted

The Tainted used to be normal children but they were brainwashed by the Chayos.

The Chayos

The Chayos are robots that have taken over Earth. They want to find the Helix. Will the Helix defeat them?

Guardians

Noah and Harmony are the guardians of the Helix.

The Story...

Mato and Shak are trapped in the Mind Sweep room! Can they escape or will they be brainwashed like the Tainted? Kes is with Abe, Harmony and Noah's friend, but can she find Mato and Shak in time?

The Helix and their guardians go to a hanger. Abe is there.

Time to go!

Everyone runs onto the ship. Abe flies it away.
I can't believe we got away.
We're so happy you're safe.
Harmony... who is the fourth Helix?
TO BE CONTINUED...

Level Up...

Answer the questions below. Each correct answer gains you points. Are you a Trainee or a Grand Master?

1 *Multiple Choice:*
The Mind Sweep makes Mato feel...
a) Different
b) The same
c) Sick

1pt

2 *Multiple Choice:*
Who do Shak and Mato go to find?
a) Kes
b) The Chayos
c) The Tainted

1pt

3 What was Abe's experiment for?

2pts

4 *Fill in the sentence:*
Let's use these _____ to talk to each other.

3pts

6 *Multiple Choice:*
In the end, how do the Helix escape with their guardians, Harmony and Noah? **1pt**
a) They ride away on Mato's back
b) Abe finds a ship for them
c) They sneak out of the city

Answers on the next page. Every correct answer earns points (pts) Which level are you?

Level:
0 - 1pts = Trainee
2 - 4pts = Novice
5 - 7pts = Adept
8 - 9pts = Expert
10pts = Grand Master

Explore...

Think about what happens next.

- How do you think Harmony and Noah feel to be free from the Chayos?

- Where do you think the fourth Helix could be?

- Is Abe trustworthy? Were Harmony and Noah happy to see him?

Other Titles

AS Geography
UNIT 1

AQA

Specification A

Module 1: Core Concepts in Physical Geography

Steve Cooper

Philip Allan Updates
Market Place
Deddington
Oxfordshire
OX15 0SE

tel: 01869 338652
fax: 01869 337590
e-mail: sales@philipallan.co.uk
www.philipallan.co.uk

© Philip Allan Updates 2001
First published January 2001
Revised October 2001, April 2002
ISBN 0 86003 461 5

This Guide has been written specifically to support students preparing for the AQA Specification A AS Geography Unit 1 examination. The content has been neither approved nor endorsed by AQA and remains the sole responsibility of the author.

Typeset by Magnet Harlequin, Oxford
Printed by Information Press, Eynsham, Oxford

Contents

Introduction

■ ■ ■

Content Guidance

■ ■ ■

Questions and Answers

Introduction

About this guide

This guide is for students following the AQA Specification A AS Geography course. It aims to guide you through Unit 1, which examines the content of **Module 1: Core Concepts in Physical Geography**.

This guide will clarify:
- the content of the module so that you know and understand what you have to learn
- the nature of the unit test
- the geographical skills and techniques that you will need to know for the assessment
- the standards you will need to reach to achieve a particular grade
- the examination techniques you will require to improve your performance and maximise your achievement

This introduction describes the structure of AS Geography and outlines the aims of Module 1. It then provides an explanation of some of the key command words used in examination papers. There is also advice concerning geographical skills, and learning and revision techniques.

The Content Guidance section summarises the essential information of Module 1. It is designed to make you aware of the material that has to be covered and learnt. In particular, the meaning of key terms is made clear.

The Question and Answer section provides sample questions and candidate responses at C-grade level and at A-grade level. Each answer is followed by a detailed examiner's response. It is suggested that you read through the relevant topic area in the Content Guidance section before attempting a question from the Question and Answer section, and only read the specimen answers after you have tackled the question yourself.

AS Geography

The AS is a new examination. It has been established as an intermediate standard between GCSE and A-level, the standard being defined as that which candidates have reached at the end of one year of study of an A-level course. Candidates may decide to continue to study for another year to take the A-level, which will be maintained at the traditional A-level standard. The AS is therefore a free–standing qualification but is also part of A-level.

All students taking the AS Geography examination for this specification (syllabus) must study Module 1 (which is one of three compulsory modules) and take the examination at the appropriate time. It is one of the six modules that contribute to the full A-level qualification. The structure of the qualification and the unit weightings for AQA Specification A are set out below.

AS

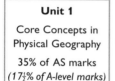
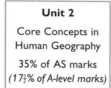
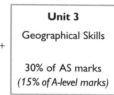

Unit 1		Unit 2		Unit 3		AS Geography
Core Concepts in Physical Geography	+	Core Concepts in Human Geography	+	Geographical Skills	=	
35% of AS marks		35% of AS marks		30% of AS marks		
(17½% of A-level marks)		(17½% of A-level marks)		(15% of A-level marks)		

A-level (AS plus the following)

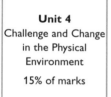

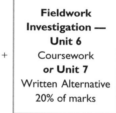

Unit 4		Unit 5		Fieldwork Investigation — Unit 6		A-level Geography
Challenge and Change in the Physical Environment	+	Challenge and Change in the Human Environment	+	Coursework or Unit 7 Written Alternative	=	
15% of marks		15% of marks		20% of marks		

The aims of Module 1

This first module of the AS course aims to help you:
- learn and apply knowledge and understanding of physical processes
- understand the effects people have on these processes and the effects the processes have on people
- apply this knowledge and understanding at at least two scales
- develop an understanding of the relationships between people and their environments
- learn and apply geographical skills
- understand that geography is dynamic
- reflect the importance of people's values and attitudes to issues and questions

Understanding these aims will be even more important to those of you who wish to continue on to A-level. A-level includes the requirement for candidates to be aware of 'synopticity'. This means that you must be able to apply your knowledge and understanding to demonstrate the links between the different parts of the geography specification. So the modules you study at AS are relevant to your A-level answers and should not be forgotten or discarded!

Examination skills

Before looking at typical examination questions and responses in the Question and Answer section, we will examine the broader skills that are essential for success in the examination. These fall into two areas: understanding the command words; and making the most effective use of the examination paper.

The importance of command words

Command words are used by the examiners to tell you what to do in order to answer examination questions effectively. The words are set out below, in an approximate order of difficulty and skill level, with an explanation of what they mean.

Command word(s)	Meaning
Describe...	State simply what is requested. Explanation or further comment is not required.
Name/State...	Identify briefly. One word may be adequate, but it may be better to use a sentence if in any doubt.
Distinguish between...	Define and state the differences between. Linking terms, such as 'whereas' or 'on the other hand', are essential.
Outline...	Describe, with a specific focus, the geographical element requested. For example, 'Outline the main features of ...' has more of a focus than 'Describe the main features of ...'
Outline the reasons for...	Give reasons for, with a specific focus, the geographical element required. The response will be briefer than a full explanation.
Account for/ Explain/Why...?	Give reasons for. The marks will be awarded for these reasons, rather than for description.
Give reason(s) for...	Some explanation must be offered.
Describe and explain...	Both elements, description and explanation, must be present for full marks. Ensure that examples of the mentioned theme are used in the response.
Compare...	What are the similarities between? Some element of contrast may be present.
Contrast...	What are the differences between? Two separate accounts will not meet the needs of this command; there must be a specific contrast or distinction between the elements.
Examine...	Give an overview of the elements which affect the theme, i.e. outline *and* explain.
Assess/to what extent...?	This requires an assessment of the importance of the factors involved in the response. This would be in an extended prose answer, rather than a short one.

The unit test

Module 1 is assessed by Unit 1. You have 1 hour to answer this paper, which accounts for 35% of the AS Geography qualification. The paper is divided into four sections: short-answer questions in Sections A, B and C and extended prose questions in Section D.

Sections A–C

In Sections A–C, there are six short-answer questions, two from each of the three elements: (1) Water on the land, (2) Climatic hazards and change, and (3) Energy and life. You have to answer one question only from two of the three sections.

Each question is marked out of 15, so there are 30 marks for the short-answer questions, out of 70 for the whole paper. You are advised to spend 30 minutes on Sections A–C. This means you have about 15 minutes per question. The spacing on the short-answer questions allows two lines per mark for your response, which is written in the question book. It is therefore useful to allocate your time accordingly. The highest number of marks is for the last part, so you should allow half the time on each question for this — about 7–8 minutes. Try to keep within the lines allocated, but if this proves to be impossible, use the lined pages at the end of the question booklet, making sure that you have clearly indicated what you have done and have identified each response.

Section D

There are three extended prose questions in Section D, one from each of the three elements of the module. You have to answer one question from the element from which you have not answered a short-answer question. For example, if you have answered a short-answer question on each of Water on the land and Climatic hazards and change, you must answer the extended prose question on Energy and life. These are marked out of 20 and then doubled to give a mark out of 40, out of a total of 70 marks for the whole paper. You are advised to spend 30 minutes on this section.

The questions are in two parts, (a) and (b), each with the same allocation of 10 marks. Therefore, equal time should be spent on each part.

Your answers are written in the question book, which has several lined pages for this purpose. (If you do not have enough sheets, additional sheets can be requested; please make sure that you attach these to the question book.)

The examiners are looking for good organisation in these answers. This should take the form of a brief introduction which sets the scene; development of the points to be made, with examples; and a brief conclusion which summarises the main points made. It helps if you have a plan in your head and jot down a number of points very briefly at the start of this type of question. Remember to check the command words so that you present the appropriate responses.

Response levels

In Sections A–C, the first two or three parts of each short-answer question are given 1 or 2 marks for each point, while the final part is marked according to Levels. There are criteria for reaching these Levels depending on the quality of the geographical content and the use of geographical and English language. These parts require a fuller development of geographical understanding and language skills.

The extended prose responses in Section D are marked using the same Levels. These are as follows.
- Level 1 (basic) responses offer one or two points without examples.
- Level 2 (clear) responses show some understanding, better use of language and make points with examples.
- Level 3 (detailed) responses show detailed understanding, make several points with examples, and use language effectively.

The command words are important, so make sure you remember to follow the instructions.

Geographical skills

As an integral part of your studies for this unit, you are required to develop a variety of skills. There are six types of geographical skill specified at AS:
- basic skills
- graphical skills
- cartographic skills
- ICT (information and communication technology) skills
- statistical skills
- investigative skills

Basic skills

Base maps
The drawing or use of photocopied base maps of a drainage basin, climatic distribution or vegetation distribution, and the use of overlays for comparison of different river basins. Annotation is an effective addition to such maps.

Sketch maps
These require you to select only relevant information to produce, for example, sketch maps of the location of hydrograph sites, management strategies in a river basin, or an urban heat island.

Atlas
The use of an atlas is essential so that global distribution of climates, biomes and soils can be identified. The atlas can also provide the basis for sketch maps.

Photographs
These are effective as an aid to interpretation, for example photographs taken of river features in the field. Other uses include the impact of climatic hazards and the characteristics of biomes.

Literacy

You need to develop literacy skills during the AS course. The assessment units require the ability to respond to both short-answer and extended prose questions.

Graphical skills

You should be familiar with the majority of these skills, but some will be new to you. You are expected to be able to interpret and construct the following.

Line graphs

Four types are specified:

- **simple line graphs**, for example hydrographs
- **comparative line graphs** — two line graphs on the same axes for comparison, for example storm hydrographs showing flashy and non-flashy rivers (you need to be aware of the use of log–log or log–normal graph paper for these graphs)
- **compound line graphs** — line graphs with amounts totalled, for example a hydrograph with the contribution of the component flows (base flow, storm flow) shown
- **divergent line graphs** — line graphs showing variation from a mean or other fixed point, which is the central horizontal axis, for example variations from the mean discharge or global temperature over a period of time

Bar graphs

Four types are specified:

- **simple bar graphs**, for example net production in biomes
- **comparative bar graphs** — bars side by side for comparison, for example to compare deforestation over time between different rainforest areas
- **compound (or divided) bar graphs** — bars divided into their components, for example the amount of discharge each tributary river contributes to the main river
- **divergent bar graphs** — bar graphs showing variation from a mean or other fixed point which is the central horizontal axis, for example variations from the mean precipitation over a period of time

Scattergraphs — and the use of the best fit line

These plot the relationship between the point data for two variables, for example flood peak discharge against time for recurrence intervals.

The best fit line is the average straight line passing between the points — the closer the points to the line, the closer the relationship between the variables. The steeper the gradient, the more rapid the change in the relationship.

There are three relationships of which you should be aware:

- **positive** — the two variables increase or decrease together and the trend of the line rises to the right, for example hydraulic radius and distance from the source of the river
- **negative** — one variable increases while the other decreases and the trend of the line falls to the right, for example discharge increasing and bedload size decreasing with distance downstream

- **no relationship** — there is no discernible trend to the pattern (this can indicate clustered data instead)

You need to be aware of the use of log–log and log–normal graph paper for scatter-graphs.

Pie charts

Pie charts use sectors of a circle to show proportions of a whole, for example the proportions of bedload particles of differing geology at a site.

Triangular graphs

These are used to show the proportions of three contributing elements, such as sand, silt and clay in a soil sample.

Lorenz curves

These show inequalities in distributions. An even distribution is shown by a straight line at 45°; the further the actual distribution is from this line, the more varied it is. Lorenz curves are not frequently used for rivers, but it would be possible to construct one to show the proportion of river flow in each continent and draw out the variation between deserts and wetter areas.

Storm hydrographs

These shows the precipitation pattern and the discharge of a river over time in response to a storm event and are covered under line graphs above.

Kite and vector diagrams

These are specialist graphs to show distribution along a transect (kite) or in a direction (vector). The former are used to show, for example, the distribution of vegetation species along a belt transect on dunes. The latter might show the orientation of prevailing winds, which influence urban climates.

Pyramids

These are used to show amounts by groups. The amount of energy found at each trophic level in an ecosystem is shown by a pyramid.

Cartographic skills

Ordnance Survey maps

You need to be familiar with these at a number of scales: 1:50 000, 1:25 000, 1:10 000 and 1:1250. You will be familiar with the smaller-scale maps from your GCSE studies, but the larger-scale maps/plans are of great value for work involving river studies. If these maps are not available in your centre, they are held in the reference sections of larger public libraries and in the planning departments of local authorities.

Soil maps

These are more specialised maps, published by the Soil Survey of Great Britain. They are usually very detailed, but you should be able to identify major podzol and brown earth soil associations. Again, these maps are often held in the reference sections of larger public libraries.

Choropleth (shading) and isoline maps

These two types of map are available for interpretation and also can be constructed from your own data.

Choropleth maps use shading to show the spatial distribution of a factor, dividing data into ranges of values represented by a different colour or texture of shading.

Isoline maps join points of equal value. Precipitation patterns (isohyets) and the velocity of water in a river channel (isovels) are two uses of these skills. Other examples include isoline maps of the distribution of soil pH values in a sample area and maps of temperature in an urban heat island (isotherms). Isoline maps show spatial changes in patterns of data.

Remember that choropleth maps should only be produced for data in the form of ratios or density and not simple numbers, whereas isolines can be used for both types of data.

ICT (information and communication technology) skills

Photographs

You need to be familiar with ground and oblique aerial photographs and be able to interpret the geographical features they depict through written answers and sketching. River channel landforms, vegetation characteristics and the effects of climatic change can be identified using photographs.

Satellite images

Land use in river basins can be identified from satellite images and used to assess land-use influences on river flooding. Areas of deforestation can also be identified.

Databases

River flow data have already been mentioned as having many uses. Climatic change data are also accessible.

Internet

This is an expanding source of information for geographers, offering an array of databases, case studies and news sources. You will not be specifically examined on this skill, though reference could be made to it. Information is available, for example, on major environmental events, river flow data and river management schemes.

Video and television programmes

You will not be specifically examined on this skill, though reference could be made to these media. Major floods and other environmental catastrophes are covered.

Statistical skills

Measures of central tendency

The **mean** is the *average* value of a set of data (arithmetic mean).

The **mode** is the *most frequently occurring* value in the data set.

The **median** is the *middle value* of the data set.

Means of dispersion

The **interquartile range** is the range between the 25th and 75th percentage points in the data set. For example, if the data listed flood events over the last 100 years, then the interquartile range would encompass the 25th highest to the 75th highest level, i.e. 25 points either side of the median. It shows the dispersion of the data from the median and thus shows the variability of flood events for a certain discharge level.

The **standard deviation (SD)** is a statistical means of assessing the average amount by which the distribution of data varies from the mean. For example, taking the situation mentioned above, the mean flood level might be 200 centimetres. An SD of 5 cm would indicate that flood levels tend to have little variation from year to year, whereas an SD of 15 cm would indicate a wider variation, as illustrated by the following table:

Mean = 200 cm	SD = 5 cm	SD = 15 cm
Within plus or minus 1 SD (68% of values)	Between 205 and 195 cm	Between 215 and 185 cm
Within plus or minus 2 SD (95% of values)	Between 210 and 190 cm	Between 230 and 170 cm
Within plus or minus 3 SD (99% of values)	Between 215 and 185 cm	Between 245 and 155 cm

In terms of the examination, you might be expected to be aware of the skill, what the results mean and to be able to carry out some simple stages of the calculations.

Correlation tests

Spearman's rank correlation coefficient is the only correlation test you need to know. This is a relatively straightforward test to establish whether a relationship exists between two sets of ranked data and what type of relationship that might be. It is used for data shown on a scattergraph (see pp. 9–10), i.e. with positive or negative relationships. The range of results is always within the range of +1.0 (perfect positive correlation) to –1.0 (perfect negative correlation). It follows that a result closer to 0 indicates a very weak relationship (more like a clustered distribution). The minimum number of pairs of data is 6 (according to statisticians), though most geographers would expect a minimum of 10 pairs to ensure a greater reliability of the result.

This test is very frequently used in river work. The relationships between velocity, discharge, bedload etc., and in terms of distance downstream, are invariably calculated by this method. The relationship between position on a slope and soil pH, moisture etc., or temperatures from the urban core are also testable by applying this skill.

In terms of the examination, you might be expected to be aware of the skill, what the results mean and to be able to carry out some simple stages of the calculations. You will not be expected to use significance at AS.

Investigative skills

The identification of geographical questions and issues

Unit 1 provides a wide range of opportunities for investigative study. Hypotheses for testing the characteristics of rivers against theory are frequently used. Examples of some simple hypotheses include 'Bedload decreases in size downstream', 'Soil pH varies with vegetation type' and 'The urban heat island is stronger under anticyclonic conditions'.

The selection of relevant primary and secondary data and an assessment of their validity

The popularity of river fieldwork means that appropriate data can be collected. The nature of the hypotheses to be tested will define the actual data collected, e.g. velocity, cross-section, wetted perimeter, bedload, discharge, gradient, infiltration rates and so on. Secondary data on river flow are available from a number of sources, including water authorities and the Environment Agency. The Internet is a valuable means of accessing such data.

You also need to understand the reliability of the methods of data collection employed and of the data collected.

The processing, presentation, analysis and interpretation of the evidence collected

These skills are developed as the course progresses and are not confined to data collected in the field. They can be assessed in a general sense in questions in Units 1 and 2 and will not be formally assessed in Unit 3. Writing up fieldwork and analysis of data downloaded from the Internet will develop such skills. In terms of rivers, soils, vegetation or climate, a comparison of the results, interpreted in relation to theory, will fulfil the requirements of this section.

The ability to draw conclusions and show an awareness of their validity

This skill is again not confined to data collected in the field. These skills could be assessed in the general sense when responding to questions in Units 1 and 2, and will not be formally assessed in Unit 3. A conclusion to and an evaluation of the success of any geographical fieldwork exercise would be appropriate here.

The awareness of risks when undertaking fieldwork

This is essential. It is not advisable to undertake fieldwork involving rivers on your own, for example. Assistance from others is needed to collect the data and to ensure your safety in any geographical fieldwork situation.

Investigative skills are best developed by a programme of fieldwork undertaken in the AS year. Preparation for work in the field, the collection of data and their interpretation and evaluation are demonstrated clearly by writing up the fieldwork in the format suggested by the board. Your teachers will be able to advise you about this.

Techniques for learning and revision

Most of you will be taking the AS examination at the end of, or during, a one-year course, with the examination taken in January or June. This means that there is no surplus time available for teaching the subject content. You must ensure that, from the start of the course, you establish good working practices to make the most of the time available.

- It is important that you do not fall behind with work during the year. New material will be taught each week so, if you are unavoidably absent (because of illness, for example), do make sure you are able to make up the missed work as quickly as possible.
- You will probably have a steady stream of homework during the course. This is likely to take a variety of forms, ranging from working from your textbook or other sources, to practising examination questions.
- Read widely from a variety of sources, including your textbook, newspapers and magazines such as *Geography Review*. Television programmes are also relevant. The information you gather will enable you to develop a number of case studies for use in your examination answers.

If you keep on top of the work, your revision programme will be more relevant and straightforward in the lead-up to exams.

The specification is divided up into modules, as we have already seen. Each module is divided into three elements and each of these into three or four sub-elements.

Module 1: Core Concepts in Physical Geography is divided as follows:

Module	Elements	Sub–elements
Core Concepts in Physical Geography	Water on the land	Systems and river regime Channel processes and landforms Flooding as a hazard River basin management
	Climatic hazards and change	Costs and benefits of weather and climate Climatic hazards Climatic change: the micro-scale Climatic change at other scales
	Energy and life	Systems, flows and cycles The time factor Soils and the impact of human activity

Revision can be more easily structured by taking the sub-elements and focusing on them. Note that it is better to revise the sub-elements in the order in which they appear, or there might be the risk that points will not make sense!

Some tips on revision

- Having selected a topic for revision, read and learn the material you have for this topic, e.g. notes, handouts, worksheets etc.
- Refer to your textbooks and to this publication. You might also find Raw, M. (2000) *AS/A-level Geography Exam Revision Notes* (Philip Allan Updates) a useful guide.
- Learn the relevant case studies. For AS you probably need no more than two for each element/sub-element and these should be at different scales to meet the examination requirements.
- Practise sample questions, keeping to the appropriate timings. Use the questions in the last section of this guide for this purpose, taking care not to look at the sample answers and examiner's comments until you have attempted the questions. There are other specimen questions available, so consult your teacher/lecturer for advice.
- Apply your knowledge and understanding when practising so that your answers reflect the demands of the question.
- Allow yourself adequate time for revision. Little and often is usually better than concentrated pressure at the last minute.

Content
Guidance

There are three elements in the specification content for Module 1:

(1) Water on the land

(2) Climatic hazards and change

(3) Energy and life

In this section, the key concepts of each of these topics are explained, together with a breakdown of what you need to know and learn.

Details of case studies are indicated under the sub-elements. One case study per sub-element is required and the scales are indicated by the following letters:

(S) Small scale (could be fieldwork)
(R) Regional scale (smaller scale than national)
(N) National scale
(G) Global scale

Points to note
- The same cases can be used for more than one sub-element, as appropriate.
- In a small number of cases, more than one case study is specified. This is indicated at the appropriate point using the code letters above. The most frequent will be comparisons of LEDW and MEDW examples.

Water on the land

Systems and river regime (S or R)

The river system and atmospheric processes

Systems are either closed or open. A closed system involves input, transfer and output of energy but not of matter, whereas an open system involves inputs and outputs of energy or matter into and from the system.

Rivers are open systems, with inputs and outputs of energy (solar radiation, evapo-transpiration) and matter (precipitation, runoff). Energy and matter are stored within the system and transferred between the stores.

This key concept involves a basic understanding of the atmospheric processes that have an influence on the river system.

Types and intensity of precipitation (frontal, orographic and convectional)
A short heavy shower leads to faster movement of water through the system, but affects only a small area; persistent precipitation will take a longer time to have an effect over the whole basin. Snow will have a delayed effect until melting occurs.

Seasonal variations in precipitation
These will influence the river regime, with wet and dry seasons having distinctive effects on the system.

You need to:
- know what a system is and how this is applied to a river
- understand the atmospheric processes that influence the system

The hydrological cycle applied to a drainage basin

A drainage basin is the area of land drained by a river. It is surrounded by higher land, the watershed. Within each drainage basin, the river system can be described by the hydrological cycle.

The hydrological cycle: definitions
- **Precipitation** — water and ice that fall from clouds into the drainage basin.
- **Interception store** — precipitation that is trapped or stored temporarily on vegetation.
- **Throughfall** — precipitation that drips from vegetation to the ground.
- **Stemflow** — precipitation that flows down plant stems to the ground.
- **Surface store** — precipitation lying on the ground.
- **Evaporation** — the change of water from liquid to gas, returning water to the atmosphere.
- **Overland flow** — the movement of water over the ground surface to a river.

- **Transpiration** — the evaporation of moisture from the stomata of plants.
- **Infiltration** — the process by which water enters the soil.
- **Soil water store** — water stored in the soil.
- **Vegetation store** — water stored in vegetation.
- **Throughflow** — water that flows through the soil to a river.
- **Percolation** — the process by which water drains to the water table.
- **Groundwater store** — water stored in the pores and crevices of rocks.
- **Groundwater flow** — water flowing in groundwater to a river.
- **Channel store** — water stored in rivers.
- **Channel flow** — water flowing in a river.
- **River runoff** — the total discharge from the river basin.

Any changes to the inputs will have an effect on the other components of the system and any changes to the components will lead to changes to others. For example, clearance of vegetation will lead to a reduction in interception, throughfall, stemflow and transpiration; an increase in surface storage and overland flow; a decrease in infiltration, soil storage, throughflow, percolation, groundwater storage and groundwater flow. Channel storage and channel flow will increase initially as water will reach the river more quickly than previously, but river runoff will remain essentially the same overall.

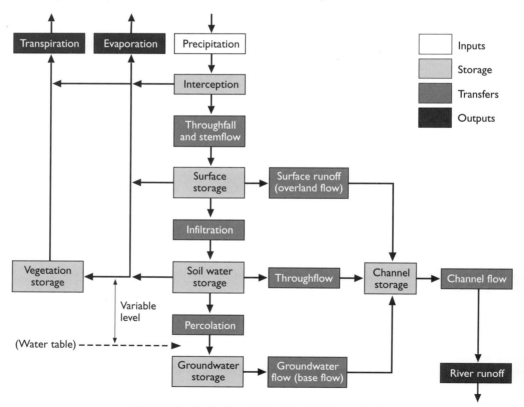

The hydrological cycle in the drainage basin

Tip Complete a blank version of the diagram, putting the components in the correct positions to see how well you understand the system.

You need to:
- be able to define a river basin and how it is identified on a map
- know the names of the components of a river system, including inputs, outputs, flows/transfers and stores
- be able to define these terms
- be able to label and interpret diagrams of the hydrological cycle
- know how changes to the inputs will affect the other components of the hydrological cycle

Annual and flood (storm) hydrographs

A hydrograph is the discharge of a river plotted on a graph. There are two types identified in geography:
- **Annual hydrographs** reflect the inputs of precipitation by type and season and the characteristics of the drainage basin, including size, shape, slope, vegetation, land use, geology and soils. Rivers that experience a distinct dry season have a very different hydrograph and river regime from rivers that have precipitation all year round. The annual hydrograph for a river in the UK starts in October, as this is the month of lowest discharge.
- **Flood (storm) hydrographs** record the response of a drainage basin to an individual precipitation event (or storm) over a short timescale.

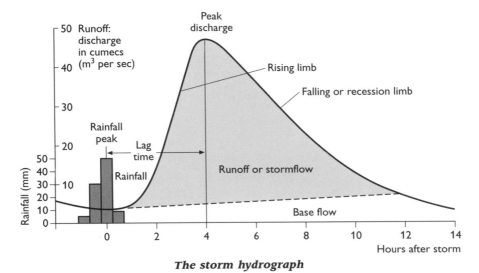

The storm hydrograph

The storm hydrograph: definitions
- **Base flow** — water that reaches the stream via groundwater flow.
- **Runoff/stormflow** — water that reaches the stream via overland flow and throughflow.

- **Peak discharge** — the time of maximum discharge after the precipitation event.
- **Rainfall peak** — the time of maximum precipitation in the precipitation event.
- **Lag time (basin lag time)** — the time between rainfall peak and peak flow.
- **Rising limb** — the increase in discharge after the start of the precipitation event.
- **Falling (recession) limb** — the decline in discharge after peak flow.
- **Discharge** — the volume of water passing a point on the river. It is calculated by multiplying the cross–sectional area (*A*) by velocity (*V*), i.e. $Q = V \times A$, and is measured in cubic metres per second (cumecs).
- **Flashy hydrograph** — one with a short lag time, with a steep rising limb and gentler, but steeper than normal, recession limb.

You need to:
- be able to define and recognise annual and flood hydrographs
- be able to define and recognise the elements of a storm hydrograph

Discharge and the drainage basin

The response of the drainage basin to a precipitation event will vary according to the relative importance of a number of factors. These factors tend to produce either a flashy hydrograph or one with a long lag time.

Factor	Shorter lag time (flashy) — higher peak and steeper rising and recession limbs	Longer lag time — lower peak and more gentle rising and recession limbs
Basin size	Smaller	Larger
Basin shape	Circular	Elongated
Relief	Steeper slopes	More gentle slopes
Type of precipitation	Intense rainfall Rapid snow melt	Prolonged rainfall Slow snow melt
Vegetation	Absent Deciduous forest in winter	Dense Deciduous forest in summer
Land use	Deforestation Farming land Desertification	Reforestation Natural vegetation Sustainable agriculture
Urbanisation	High density	Low density
Geology	Impermeable	Permeable
Soils	Clays	Sands
Drainage density	High	Low

These factors interact to produce the discharge for the individual river basin.

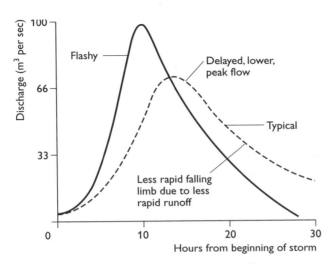

Flashy and typical hydrographs

You need to:

- identify and explain the factors that affect the shape of a hydrograph
- understand the effects of the factors that influence river discharge
- know that these factors interact with each other to produce the hydrograph shape
- understand the effects of changes to and within the hydrological cycle and their effect on the hydrograph
- apply your knowledge to one case study

The hydrograph and river flooding

The hydrograph is a summary of discharge after precipitation. Discharge will increase until the bankfull stage is exceeded. Flooding (an extreme event) is a natural process and occurs on all rivers. The conditions depend on the rate at which water reaches the river and the factors influencing the flow of water through the river system.

The frequency of a flood of a specific level is important. This is known as the recurrence (return) interval. It is found by plotting discharge against frequency and drawing the best-fit line. It can also be calculated statistically. For flood prevention, it is essential to calculate the recurrence interval for a certain level, so that, say, 50- or 100-year floods can be predicted. This will enable cost–benefit analysis to take place, as it is more cost-effective to plan flood control for a flood level that occurs frequently than for an extreme level which occurs every 100 years.

You need to:

- be aware of the links between the storm hydrograph and flooding
- be aware of the effect of extreme events on the river basin and its processes
- understand the concept of the recurrence interval and the consequences of this knowledge for people

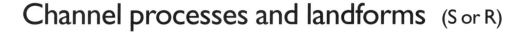

Channel processes and landforms (S or R)

Erosion, transport and deposition

Erosion: definitions
- **Abrasion (corrasion)** — the erosion of banks and river bed by bed load.
- **Corrosion (solution)** — the solution of bed and bank material.
- **Attrition** — erosion of the bedload by contact with other load, the bed and the banks.
- **Hydraulic action** — the action of the weight of water compressing air into cracks.

The rate of erosion is related to the discharge. The greatest amount of river energy and work carried out is under bankfull conditions. All the above processes increase with discharge. The size of river load decreases towards the mouth of the river as a result of attrition.

Transport: definitions
- **Suspended load** — load carried by the river in suspension.
- **Solution load** — load carried by the river in solution.
- **Saltation** — the movement of bedload by uplift and subsequent bouncing along the bed of the river.
- **Traction load** — the movement of bedload by rolling along the bed of the river.
- **Competence** — the largest particle that can be transported by a river.
- **Capacity** — the total load transported by a river.

Both competence and capacity increase as discharge increases.

The relationship between river velocity and capacity is not straightforward. Sand is transported at lower velocities than clay or pebbles as it is easy for the river to pick up sand particles; clay particles are more cohesive and pebbles are too large. The velocity required to keep particles in suspension is less than that needed to pick them up, so particles, once in motion, can remain aloft. Deposition of particles will occur with a small decrease in velocity.

Deposition
This occurs when the river has reduced energy; usually when velocity decreases. Reasons for deposition include:
- reduced precipitation and hence reduced discharge
- the river entering a lake or the sea
- a sudden increase in load
- shallower water in the river channel, either as a result of variations in the cross-section, or of discharge flooding out of the channel onto the floodplain

You need to:
- define and understand the four processes of erosion
- define and understand the processes of transportation
- define and understand the process of deposition

- understand the conditions under which these processes occur
- be aware of the factors that influence the relative importance of the processes within the channel, both in cross-section and downstream
- know the ways in which the variations in velocity and discharge affect the river's ability to erode, transport and deposit

Load

The load of a river comes from weathering on the valley slopes and the movement of this material to the river channel. It is also the result of erosion of the bed/banks of the channel. It consists of particles of varying sizes, from clay to silt, sand, gravel, pebbles, cobbles and boulders.

The type of load and where it is found will vary according to the velocity in the channel cross-profiles and long-profiles. Variations will influence channel landforms.

You need to:
- know the sources of river load
- understand where the varying types of river load are found in river channels

Landforms of river erosion and deposition

Landforms of river erosion: definitions
- **Potholes** — a rounded hole abraded by load into the resistant rock river bed.
- **Waterfall/rapids** — a sharp fall in the long profile of a river, the result of a band of resistant rock or a knickpoint. Rapids show a gentler gradient change.
- **Meander** — a sinuous section of the plan of a river. The shape changes as a result of erosion on the outside of the meander bend causing the meander to migrate. Deposition occurs on the inside of the bend.
- **Oxbow lake** — the result of erosion on the outside of a very sinuous meander. The meander neck is cut through, under flood conditions. Sediment is deposited along the new channel and the old meander loop is cut off, with water remaining as the oxbow lake.
- **Riffle** — a shallow section of the channel which occurs where velocity is lower between meander pools.
- **Pool** — a deeper section of the channel which occurs where velocity is greater on the outside of a meander bend.

Landforms of river deposition: definitions
- **Floodplain** — the area into which the river floods when bankfull stage is exceeded. The change in the river's channel cross-section causes lower competence, depositing the load. A thin layer of silt builds up with each flood.
- **Levée** — the build-up of coarser sediment at the banks of the river as it overflows its channel onto the floodplain, causing a small natural embankment. Levées are often artificially enhanced as flood-prevention measures.
- **Delta** — the result of the decrease in velocity when a river enters a lake or the sea. The coarsest sediment is deposited first and the finest last of all.

Flooding has a great effect on the formation of, and changes to, channel landforms. You need to study one river to understand the range of these landforms and how they change over time. The Mississippi is well documented, but you can study any river, possibly by personal fieldwork.

You need to:

- define and explain the main landforms associated with erosion: potholes, waterfalls/rapids, meanders and oxbow lakes
- define and explain the main landforms associated with deposition: levées, floodplains and deltas
- know how these landforms are formed and how they change with variations in discharge
- be aware of the effects of extreme events on the development of landforms
- apply this knowledge to case studies

Flooding as a hazard (R or N)

Definition of a hazard

A hazard is detrimental to people or property. It can have natural and/or human causes. Flooding is a natural event, but it is clear that there are human actions that contribute to floods. The hazard of flooding is increasing; there are more people living in areas liable to flood and there is greater human impact on the drainage basin.

Natural (physical) and human causes of flooding

Natural causes	Human causes
Intense precipitation events	Deforestation — more overland flow
Higher than average precipitation over a period of time	Urbanisation — shorter lag time as there is less infiltration
Already saturated ground when more precipitation falls	Development on floodplains
Rapid snow melt	Rapid snow melt (global warming)
Sea level rise	Sea level rise (global warming)
Storm surges (in coastal areas)	Drainage of wetlands

Flooding is caused by an increase in overland flow and a decrease in interception, infiltration, throughflow and groundwater flow. The hydrographs show a shorter lag time, the water exceeds the capacity of the channel and flooding occurs.

Urban areas produce shorter lag times, so development on floodplains increases the flood hazard. As more people live on floodplains, for example Maidenhead on the Thames and Dhaka in Bangladesh, the perception of the hazard is increasing as flooding occurs more frequently. The recurrence interval is shortening because of changes to land use. The influence of climatic change on sea levels is most important in coastal areas, such as southeast England and The Maldives.

You need to:
- know the physical causes of flooding
- understand the effects of intense precipitation events and the factors that affect the movement of water though the hydrological cycle and the drainage basin
- be aware of the ways in which human activity has increased the risk of flooding
- understand the effects of changes in land use, new settlement and climatic change

Examples of flooding as a hazard

This requires the study of cases from both the UK and from an LEDW area experiencing recurrent flooding (such as Bangladesh). Case studies are found in such publications as *Geography Review* (Derwent floods, 1999), and textbooks. You will find more recent examples in newspapers as they occur (October/November 2000). The causes of the individual flooding events can be identified.

River basin management (R or N)

Many rivers have been managed in order to control any combination of the above flood causes. Flood control is one of the most important reasons for river management, along with water supply/irrigation. Other factors influencing management include the river basin's location in terms of climate, economic and political geography and population pressure. Increasingly, political and conservation considerations are important in drainage basins that include a number of countries.

Reason	Example
Flood control	Colorado, Mississippi, Thames, Rhine
Hydro-electricity	Colorado, Nile, Rhine, Zambezi
Irrigation	Colorado, Orange, Niger
Water supply	Colorado, Rhine, Thames
Recreation	Colorado, Rhine, Thames
Navigation	Mississippi, Rhine, Thames

You need to:
- understand the definition of multipurpose schemes and river basin management
- be aware of the reasons for river basin management

Strategies of river basin management

The strategies and responses range in scale, with contrasts evident between the LEDW (e.g. the Ganges) and the MEDW (e.g. the Colorado). A number of river basins are becoming important politically. Case studies could include the Colorado, Jordan, Tigris and Euphrates or Ganges, all of which cross international boundaries.

It will be important to cover the examples required, but also to reduce these to a minimum. Two cases are needed. In practice, it may be preferable to use one pair of cases (e.g. LEDW — Ganges; MEDW — Colorado) to cover both flooding as a hazard and strategies of river basin management.

Direct (hard engineering)	Indirect (soft engineering)
Dams	Afforestation
Barrages	Agricultural land-use management
River channel management	Urban land-use management
Flood compensation reservoirs	Urban development controls
	Flood warning systems

These strategies should be applied to your case studies in terms of which have been or which could be applied.

You need to:
- know the strategies of river management from your case studies
- be aware of both direct and indirect strategies from your case studies
- study cases from both MEDW and LEDW examples to demonstrate the comparisons and contrasts in responses and strategies

The costs and benefits of river basin management

The costs and benefits of water management schemes include socio-economic, environmental and political factors:

Benefits	Costs
Flood control	Loss of land — displacement of people
Agricultural water supply	Increase in water-borne disease
Urban water supply	Financial costs/debt
Recreation	Less effective navigation because of dams
Improved navigation	Environmental damage
Hydro-electricity	Water abstraction greater than flow downstream — river may not reach the sea
Economic growth	Increased erosion downstream
Conservation areas created	Sedimentation shortens life of dam
	Salinisation — higher salt content in water — affects agriculture and fauna
	Lower oxygen in water below dam affects fauna
	Political implications for international river management — may lead to conflict in certain cases

The benefits are important at the time of construction and the costs, particularly environmental and political, become more apparent after the completion of the schemes. You must apply an analysis of costs and benefits to a case study. Some river basin management schemes are more successful than others; you must also be able to evaluate the success of the strategies used and any issues that result.

You need to:
- be aware of the socio-economic, environmental and political costs and benefits of a case study from the MEDW and the LEDW
- consider and evaluate river basin management strategies
- know that there are variations in the effectiveness of different river management schemes

River management and sustainable development

All river basin management schemes have costs and benefits. Sustainable development means that the needs of the present are met, without causing problems in the future. River basin management schemes should not cause deterioration in the environment, economy or resource availability for future generations. Questions that need to be asked are:
- have schemes been effective to date?
- what will they be like in 50 years?
- will they be as effective in the future?
- what procedures will ensure that effectiveness is maintained, and should these be implemented?

You need to:
- be able to define sustainable development
- consider the relationships between river basin management and sustainable development

Climatic hazards and change
Costs and benefits of weather and climate (R or N)

The global distribution of climates

Climate is defined as the average long-term weather conditions for an area. Weather is defined as the current conditions of the atmosphere at a local scale. There is a pattern to the world distribution of climates. This is influenced by solar radiation, the distribution of land and sea, ocean currents, prevailing winds, altitude, temperature and precipitation.

You need to:
- have an understanding of the broad distribution of world climates
- know in outline the factors that have influenced this pattern

Tropical monsoon (TM) and cool temperate western maritime (CTWM) climates and their characteristics

You must study these two climatic types, know where they are found and be able to locate them on a world map. You must be able to discuss the characteristics of the climates, including the temperature and precipitation patterns by season, and understand the factors that lead to these characteristics.

Characteristic	Tropical monsoon	Cool temperate western maritime
Temperature	High all year; range greater	Warmer in summer, cooler in winter; smaller range
Precipitation	Summer rainfall, winter drought; mostly convectional and orographic	Occurs all year round; frontal, convectional and orographic
Winds	Offshore in winter; onshore in summer	Westerly prevailing
Pressure systems	High in winter; low in summer	Lower in winter, higher in summer, but can vary greatly
Air masses	Tropical maritime in summer; polar continental in winter; meet at inter-tropical convergence zone (ITCZ)	Mostly tropical maritime and polar maritime; meet at polar front Also experiences tropical and polar continental and arctic maritime

You need to:
- understand the environmental control and atmospheric processes which are responsible for the characteristics of these climate types
- be able to compare and contrast the causal factors of these climate types

Opportunities and constraints for people

Both of these climates provide opportunities and constraints for human activities. Agriculture, water management, tourism, flooding and drought are the main areas of interaction.

Each climate affects people in different ways and the responses reflect the level of economic development.

These opportunities and constraints are dependent on seasonal and spatial variations. For example, the monsoon is typified by wet and dry seasons and the effects of mountains; the western maritime climate by warm summers and cool winters with more precipitation in winter; mountains are an important influence on precipitation.

Case studies at a regional level are essential. Northwest Europe (CTWM) and the Indian sub-continent (TM) are good case studies to demonstrate and contrast these climates.

You need to:

- have an understanding of the opportunities for and constraints on human activity in areas experiencing both of these climatic types
- be aware of variations in the climatic pattern, in both space and time
- have studied example case studies of both climatic types. These need to be at the regional scale, i.e. as areas, rather than by national boundaries
- integrate the location of the climate type, its characteristics and causal factors and the opportunities for, and constraints on, human activity

Climatic hazards (R or N)

Climatic hazards occur as short-term weather conditions. There are two main types for study here: strong wind and drought.

The definition of a hazard has been covered under flooding above.

You need to:

- be able to define a climatic hazard
- be aware of the types of climatic hazard and how these are classified

Strong wind

There are three hazards identified here: severe gales, tropical revolving storms (including hurricanes) and tornadoes. All are products of intense pressure gradients.

Severe gales are associated with deep depressions in mid-latitudes. The strongest winds occur with the passing of warm and cold fronts, although any part of the depression can experience such winds. The great storm of 1987 in southeast England is a case in point. These storms can be very destructive and cause coastal flooding.

Tropical revolving storms develop from troughs of low pressure in the easterly winds. Under certain conditions they can develop into hurricanes: 5°–20° of latitude away from the equator, with a sea surface temperature of more than 26°C in autumn (maximum sea temperature) so that (usually) large amounts of water vapour condense and release latent heat. They dissipate over land or outside the tropics. These storms have strong winds, intense precipitation, and can cause coastal storm surges, flooding and landslides; they are up to 400 km across. Hurricanes are a seasonal annual event and a recent case study is usually available.

Tornadoes occur at cold fronts in summer at the meeting of cold dry polar air and warm moist tropical air. They have a very low central pressure, very strong winds and are extremely destructive. They are very short-lived (20 minutes on average), are 100–400 metres wide and travel at 50–90 kilometres per hour. Tornado Alley in the USA provides an annual case study.

You need to:

- understand strong winds, including severe gales, tropical revolving storms (including hurricanes) and tornadoes
- locate the parts of the world in which these hazards occur
- identify the characteristics of each of these hazards
- be able to explain the causes of each of these hazards

Drought

Drought is a hazard in many parts of the world. It is an *abnormal* condition, and should not be confused with an annual dry season. The Sahel in Africa is specified for study. The causes of drought in this area are both natural and human, including rainfall variability in amount and reliability, desertification and the disruptive effects of war. The variable movement of the ITCZ at the meeting of dry continental and moist maritime air masses should be understood. The air masses and atmospheric conditions that cause drought in the UK should be known.

You need to:

- be able to define drought
- study the Sahel zone in Africa
- know and understand the atmospheric processes and air masses responsible for drought

The impact of hazards

The impact of the hazards studied in this section varies in different parts of the world. It depends on the level of economic development (MEDC or LEDC), cultural perceptions and the intensity of the hazard itself. Study of the contrasts between MEDCs and LEDCs in terms of the impact of the hazard and the responses to the hazard event is essential. Case studies at regional or national scales are required.

A number of these hazards occur every year. Tornadoes and hurricanes/cyclones are reported in the news (e.g. Hurricane Mitch) while textbooks contain older examples, such as the 1987 storm in southeast England and Hurricane Hugo. The impact of these events and the responses to them are usually reported in the media as they occur.

You need to:

- know that the impact of these hazards varies in different parts of the world
- know that responses to these hazards vary in different parts of the world
- be aware that there are different impacts and responses arising from variations in culture, the level of economic development and the intensity of the hazard event
- compare and contrast impacts and responses in the MEDW and the LEDW
- study cases of impact and response at the regional or national scale

Climatic change: the micro-scale (S)

Small-scale climatic change occurs in urban areas. The effects are more marked in larger urban areas and include modifications in temperature, humidity, precipitation, winds and air quality.

Parameter	Effects	Cause
Temperature	Higher within urban margin, increasing towards centre; best observed under anticyclonic conditions just before dawn	Solar radiation absorbed and released from buildings; central heating energy released from buildings
Humidity	Lower in urban areas	Higher urban temperatures; less transpiration from vegetation
Precipitation	Higher in large urban areas; higher downwind of urban area; less snow, frost; more fog	More convection due to heating; more particulate matter allows precipitation to develop; higher temperatures;
Winds	Lower velocity, but more turbulence; increase in funnelling	Effects of rougher urban landscape due to buildings of different heights; modern buildings make narrow passageways for wind
Air quality	Lower — photochemical smog	More particulate matter; more pollution from internal combustion engines
Sunlight	Lower	More cloud; more particulate matter reflects radiation

You need to:
- be aware of the types of change of climate that occur at a small scale in urban areas
- know and understand how and why the urban landscape can modify temperature, humidity, precipitation, winds and air quality
- know and understand the urban heat island, patterns of humidity influenced by variations in density of land use, the effects of buildings on temperature and radiation, the effects of buildings on wind speeds (including channelling) and air quality

Urban air pollution

The main type of urban air pollution is now photochemical smog (caused by exhaust gases and hydrocarbons from motor vehicles plus the effects of sunlight). The ideal weather conditions for the formation of photochemical smogs are anticylonic, where the pollution cannot escape because of an inversion. Radiation at night causes the air in contact with the ground to be cooled, which prevents the escape of pollution because the unpolluted air above is warmer.

You need to:
- be able to define photochemical smog
- be aware of the causes of smog

- know the atmospheric processes that contribute to the formation of smog
- know the human activities responsible for the formation of smog
- have studied one case study

The effects on people

Urban air quality changes have an impact on people. Pollution causes respiratory illnesses, in particular. Lead from car exhausts also affects people. For many years, measures have been taken by governments to reduce the effects of air pollution.

Hazard	Strategies
Photochemical smog	Use of catalytic converters; strategies to reduce the use of cars — road charging, fuel taxes, public transport priority lanes, restrictions by days of the week, car sharing
Lead	No longer used in car fuel

The success of these policies should be considered.

Photochemical smog is a growing issue as the use of the car is increasing in most urban areas. Although the problems are well known and understood, there is a reluctance by motorists to give up this freedom of movement. The government currently has a number of policies under review, but has not resolved the dilemma. Any restriction on the use of the motor car involves personal values and attitudes and such issues are not easy to resolve.

You need to:
- know and understand the impact changes in air quality have had on human activity, including effects on health, the economy and society
- have studied the responses and strategies that have been employed to alleviate the effects of these changes
- use one case study
- evaluate the success of the strategies employed in the case study
- analyse the attitudes and values of decision-makers in considering this issue (e.g. what are the competing viewpoints?)

Climatic change at other scales (G)

El Niño southern oscillation (ENSO) and La Niña

El Niño is an event that occurs every 2–9 years. It is the result of unusually high sea temperatures in the eastern Pacific which cause the reversal of the normal westward flow of trade winds and ocean currents.

La Niña occurs when abnormally cool water is at the surface of the eastern Pacific and is associated with stronger than normal trade winds. The southern oscillation refers to this see-sawing of conditions, notably of atmospheric pressure over the eastern and western tropics. Under 'normal' conditions pressure rises over the eastern Pacific and falls over Indonesia. El Niño is a reversal of this pattern.

You need to:
- know about and be able to define ENSO and La Niña
- be able to distinguish El Niño from La Niña
- know, in outline, the causes of the features

Climatic and economic consequences of ENSO

Climatic consequences	Economic consequences
Drier conditions and possibly drought occurring in Indonesia and northern Australia	Impact on agriculture, forest fires, smog pollution
Increased rainfall in the eastern Pacific	Flooding, landslides
Increased occurrence of violent storms and hurricanes	Impact on agriculture and tourism
Late arrival of the monsoon in southeast Asia	Impact on agriculture
Warmer water in the eastern Pacific	Decline of fishing in Peru

You need to:
- know the climatic and economic effects of ENSO in the Pacific Basin   (R)

Global warming

Global warming is a consequence of the greenhouse effect. The greenhouse gases (water vapour, carbon dioxide, CFCs, methane and nitrogen oxides, in decreasing importance) absorb long-wave radiation from the Earth and thus prevent it from escaping into space. This raises the Earth's temperature. In recent years this natural process has been accelerated by these gases as they are all (except water vapour) increasing in the atmosphere as a result of human activity.

Greenhouse gas	Source
Water vapour	Evaporation, transpiration
Carbon dioxide	Respiration, burning of fossil fuels, deforestation and burning
CFCs (chlorofluorocarbons)	Aerosols, refrigerators
Methane	Decaying vegetation, landfill, cattle
Nitrogen oxides	Fertilisers, vehicle exhausts

You need to:
- be able to define global warming
- know the greenhouse gases, their origins and their relative importance
- be aware that some greenhouse gases are of natural origin and some are of human origin
- be able to explain why global warming is of increasing importance, although the evidence is challenged by some authorities

The effects on climate and people

The actual impact of global warming on any one area is open to some conjecture, depending on the computer model used. Some of the possible impacts on the UK and an LEDC are set out in the table below.

UK	Bangladesh (LEDC)
Warmer and wetter; seasonal rainfall stronger; more like a Mediterranean climate; alternatively, other models emphasise increased rainfall all year	Increase in storms and cyclones (hurricanes)
Coastal flooding increases as sea level rises due to expansion of water in the oceans with higher temperatures; this will cause displacement of population, industry and agriculture	Increased flooding as sea level rises due to expansion of water in the oceans with higher temperatures; this will cause displacement of population (most of the country is only a few metres above current sea levels)
Changes to crops; more maize and Mediterranean-type crops	Longer wet season; longer growing season
Water supply problems in summer	More variability in the monsoon; negative impact on agriculture
Increased disease and pests — malarial mosquitoes, brown-tailed moth (causes an itching rash)	Economic costs too great for country to respond

You need to:
- know the effects of global warming on the climate of the UK and one LEDC
- include effects on weather (warmer, wetter or drought), coastal areas as sea levels rise, agriculture and general plant growth, and on animal distribution

Political responses to global warming

There are a number of responses to this issue being undertaken by governments, though the level of response depends on a country's circumstances. The Maldive Islands, for example, are very concerned as their land is only a few metres above sea level. The USA, on the other hand, is heavily dependent on fossil fuels and does not see global warming as a serious enough issue to necessitate a cut-back on fuel consumption, though it is offering to plant forests in order to absorb carbon dioxide from the atmosphere.

There have been three major global conferences to coordinate strategies in recent years: the Earth Summit of 1992 (energy saving); the Montreal Protocol of 1986 (CFC reduction); and the Kyoto Summit of 1998 (energy reduction to reduce the use of fossil fuels). The use of CFCs has declined very rapidly and substitutes are in place. However, there has been little progress globally in the reduction of the burning of fossil fuels. The UK government has agreed to reduce the output of carbon dioxide by 50% by 2010, but the US takes a different view. Countries in the LEDW are also concerned that proposals to reduce carbon dioxide will restrict their economic growth and perpetuate the dominance of the MEDW.

The most common strategies to tackle global warming include limitations on the use of fossil fuels; the use of alternative energy sources; increased fuel efficiency; controls on deforestation; afforestation; and the international agreements mentioned above.

You need to:
- be aware of the strategies currently employed to reduce the impact of global warming
- be able to evaluate the effectiveness of such strategies
- know about the political responses to global warming including the Montreal Protocol and the Earth Summit
- be aware of and understand the values and attitudes underlying these varying political responses

Think globally, act locally

This issue brings out the concepts of sustainable development and global interdependence. These relate to the interrelationships between the LEDW and the MEDW in terms of trade, investment, aid and migration. The relationship is frequently seen as one-sided, but there can be benefits for both sides. In this case, global warming cannot be tackled without the cooperation of all countries. However, the individual can make a difference by following a sustainable lifestyle, which reduces the use of energy and greenhouse gases. Recycling, walking, cycling, using public transport etc. are all examples of individual decisions, which collectively can make a contribution.

You need to:
- be able to define sustainable development and global interdependence
- understand the relationships between the two concepts to include the potential impact of global warming on economic development in LEDCs and MEDCs
- be aware of your own values in relation to global warming — this could include your own attitudes towards consumption and recycling, public versus private transport, the use of fossil or renewable fuels etc.
- consider the concept 'think globally, act locally'

Energy and life

Systems, flows and cycles (S/G)

Ecosystems and biomes

An ecosystem is defined as a living system of plants and animals which interacts with the physical environment. On the other hand, a biome is defined as a major climax community of plants and animals which has reached equilibrium with the environment.

An ecosystem consists of biotic (living) and abiotic (non-living) components. The biotic component comprises plants and animals; the abiotic component comprises soils, air, water etc.

You need to:
- know the definitions of 'ecosystem' and 'biome' and be able to distinguish between them
- be able to define the terms 'biotic' and 'abiotic'

Energy flows through an ecosystem

Energy flows through an ecosystem from one trophic level to another. The initial source of energy is the sun. This energy is converted into plant matter by photosynthesis. At each trophic level 90% of energy is lost at transfer by respiration, excretion, decomposition and heat loss. This means that a smaller number of species can be supported at the next trophic level. The components are summarised in the table below.

Trophic level			Example	Energy %
4	Omnivores	Tertiary consumers	Fox	0.1
3	Carnivores	Secondary consumers	Weasel	1
2	Herbivores	Primary consumers	Vole	10
1	Plants	Autotrophs or producers	Grass	100
Input	Solar energy			

Decomposers (bacteria and fungi) operate at all trophic levels, as do detritivores (e.g. worms and other soil fauna) which break down dead organic material).

The movement of energy up the trophic levels demonstrates the food chain, a simple way of describing the order in which species feed on each other. A food chain is demonstrated in the 'Example' column of the table above. In reality, the relationships are more complex as some species can occupy more than one position; for example, the vole is eaten by a variety of species, which in turn can be prey for other carnivores and omnivores. This arrangement is called a 'food web'.

You need to:

- know the inputs, flows and outputs of energy
- define and explain the concept of trophic levels
- be aware of the consequences of the energy losses at each level
- be able to define and explain the roles of producers (autotrophs), consumers (herbivores, carnivores, omnivores) and detritivores
- understand food chains and food webs and the flow of energy through them
- study an ecosystem at a small-scale by fieldwork or other means

Nutrients are cycled in an ecosystem

Nutrients are essential for the production of organic material and are recycled continuously. Plants take up nutrients from the air and from the soil water. The inputs come from weathered rock and the atmosphere; the outputs are leaching from the soil and the removal of organic matter from the ecosystem. The most important nutrients are carbon, nitrogen, phosphorus and sulphur. There are many others, called trace elements, including aluminium, iron and sodium. These are taken up by plants, passed on to herbivores, carnivores and omnivores, and then detritivores reduce them to their original state by decomposition back into the soil.

The carbon cycle is illustrated in the following diagram:

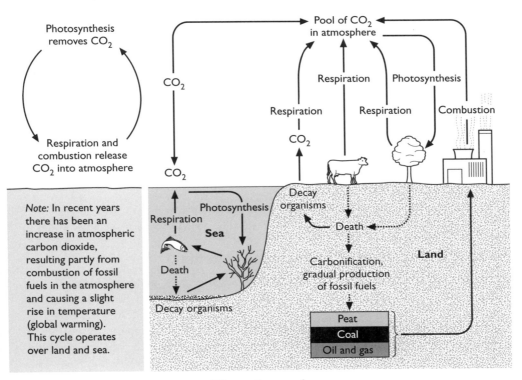

The carbon cycle

Within an ecosystem, nutrients are held in three nutrient stores: litter, biomass and soil. In tropical rainforest, the largest store is in the biomass, with the soil next and litter the smallest. In temperate grassland, the largest store is in the soil, followed by the biomass and then the litter. This reflects the temperature, rainfall and other environmental conditions influencing the ecosystems. The nutrients are transferred between the stores as part of the cycling process.

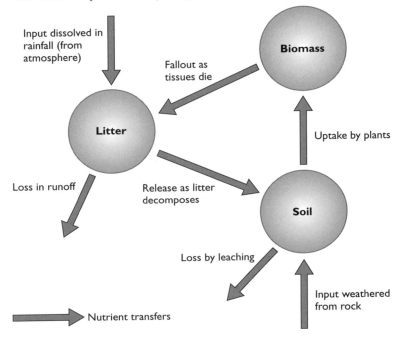

The mineral nutrient cycle

You need to:

- know the inputs, flows and outputs of nutrients
- study one example of nutrient cycling out of the carbon, nitrogen, phosphorus or sulphur cycles
- know and understand the nutrient stores and transfers between them
- study an ecosystem at a small scale — this could be done by fieldwork or other means

Productivity varies between ecosystems

The productivity of an ecosystem is the amount of organic material produced. It is measured in dry grammes per square metre per year. The net productivity is the primary production less respiration ($N = P - R$). Productivity varies between ecosystems because of variations in solar radiation, precipitation, latitude, temperature and length of growing season. Many natural ecosystems are more productive than agricultural ones as they maximise the use of solar energy (agricultural ecosystems have bare ground and organic matter is removed in the harvest).

You should be able to explain the productivity of the ecosystems/biomes in the table below in terms of the factors mentioned above.

Biome/ecosystem	Net primary productivity (g/m²/yr)
Tropical rainforest	2200
Deciduous woodland	1200
Tropical grassland	900
Coniferous forest	800
Mediterranean	700
Agricultural	650
Temperate grassland	600
Lakes and rivers	400
Tundra	140
Oceans	125
Deserts	90

You need to:
- be able to define the productivity of an ecosystem
- understand the factors that affect the productivity of an ecosystem, including latitude, insolation, water, temperature and length of growing season
- select one biome as your case study — this can be any biome   (G)
- be able to compare and contrast productivity in both natural and agricultural systems
- study the impact of farming on natural ecosystems, including the effects on energy and nutrients

The time factor (S or R/N)

Succession and climatic climax

Time is an important factor in the development of ecosystems. A sere is a community of plants that forms a stage in the development of vegetation over a period of time. The complete sequence of seres, from the initial colonisation by pioneer communities to the climatic climax, is known as a prisere. The climatic climax vegetation is best adapted to the climatic conditions and is dominant over a large area (as in a biome). In reality, other factors, such as soils, drainage and relief, also have an impact and polyclimax is a more appropriate term. There are four priseres: lithosere (bare rock), psammosere (sand), halosere (salt water) and hydrosere (fresh water).

A typical prisere (lithosere) might consist of the following sequence of seres:

algae/bacteria – lichens/liverworts – herbs/grasses/small flowering species – ferns/bracken/small shrubs/brambles – large shrubs/small trees – large trees.

You need to:
- be able to define and understand the concepts of succession and climatic climax
- study one example of a prisere, such as a lithosere, psammosere, hydrosere or halosere

Human impact — secondary succession

People interfere with primary succession. The break in succession, if maintained, is a plagio-climax. Grazed chalk downland is a good example. However, if the break in succession is natural it is a sub-climax. Some causes are listed in the table below.

Sub-climax	Plagio-climax
Fire (lightning)	Grazing
Periodic, repeated flooding	Overgrazing
Mudflow	Deforestation
Landslide	Afforestation
Poor natural drainage (waterlogging)	Fire (deliberate)
Volcanic ash/lava flows	Agriculture

If succession restarts after a sub-climax or plagio-climax, it is secondary succession. The clearance of the rainforests over centuries has established secondary forest in much of southeast Asia. The succession that occurred after the 1883 eruption on Krakatoa is also secondary.

Relevant case studies include the effects of human intervention on deciduous woodland and of acid rain on forests in northwest Europe, as well as pollution of aquatic ecosystems in the UK.

You need to:
- define and understand the concepts of secondary succession, sub-climax and plagio-climax
- study these in terms of the human impact on deciduous woodland in northwest Europe
- study these in terms of the impact of acid rain on vegetation in northwest Europe

Deforestation

Deforestation occurs for a number of reasons, including physical, economic, social and political/cultural factors. The main example for study is the tropical rainforest. Deforestation has occurred, and is still occurring, at a rapid rate; examples include Amazonia and Indonesia. One case must be studied to allow analysis of the physical, economic, social and cultural factors which have resulted in the current situation.

If Amazonia is selected, you must consider the impact on, and interests of, the indigenous population and the new settlers. These interests are not usually compatible and are affected by the interests of those far away from the forests.

Reasons for deforestation	Consequences	Response
Subsistence agriculture	Indigenous population uses slash and burn techniques — produces secondary forest; ecosystem remains generally in balance	System in balance, but as population pressure increases, deterioration occurs
Agriculture	Forest cleared for new settlers; soil erosion, loss of biomass/ nutrients, especially potassium; contribution to global warming; loss of fertility causes land to be abandoned after a few years	Government defends policy of giving land to new settlers as part of transmigration policy to ease pressure on the towns and other, poorer, rural areas (e.g. Amazonia, Indonesia)
Ranching	Forest cleared for commercial cattle ranching; same effects on soils and environment as agriculture	Transnational corporations (TNCs) blamed for causing deforestation, e.g. McDonald's; this is denied; increasing involvement of non-governmental organisations (NGOs) and environmental groups such as Greenpeace and Friends of the Earth
Logging and woodpulp	Originally, this was selective for widely scattered species, but now wholesale clearance is needed for the same result; unwanted timber is left to rot or used for MDF; same effects on soils and environment as agriculture	As above; in addition, sustainable policies increasingly applied; replanting now occurs; MEDCs will no longer accept supplies unless from sustainable sources, both by legislation and by consumer demand
Mining	Dramatic impact on landscape; causes severe soil erosion and water pollution	Little response from national governments either in country of origin or in country of receipt as metals are needed; country has valuable source of income; role of TNCs crucial here; some campaigns are developing in MEDCs (e.g. Shell Oil production in Nigeria)

You need to:
- understand the various causes of deforestation, including physical, economic, social and political/cultural factors
- study the impact of deforestation in the tropical rainforests, including physical, economic, social and cultural factors in relation to both new settlers and the indigenous population
- select one case study, such as Indonesia or Amazonia

Values and attitudes
It is clear that the number of vested interests involved in deforestation is great. The level of economic and political power that each one has also varies, both within and outside the country. Values and attitudes to deforestation also vary.

Your own attitudes and values, even at a distance from events, can have an influence. Your consumer choices have an effect on sales of timber, fast foods and species at risk of extinction. Some people become members of Greenpeace or Friends of the Earth and actively support the aims of these pressure groups.

You need to:

- analyse and understand the values and attitudes expressed by interested parties, including those of indigenous people, settlers, governments, international agencies (UN, World Bank), NGOs and pressure groups (Greenpeace, Oxfam, Friends of the Earth)
- analyse your own values and attitudes regarding this issue

Soils and the impact of human activity (S or R/N)

Factors in soil formation

Soils are the result of interaction among animal, mineral and organic components. The main factors of soil formation are parent material, climate, relief, organisms and time.

Soils are divided into horizons. These horizons are distinctive in terms of their characteristics: texture, structure, acidity, organic content and water content. The following diagram of an ideal soil profile shows the characteristics and definitions of each horizon.

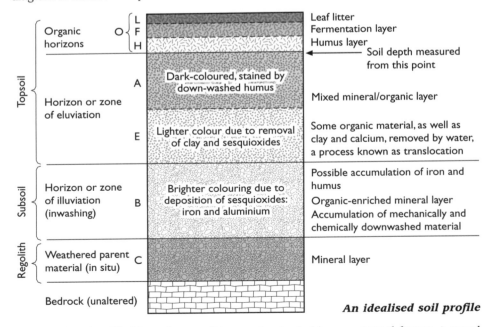

An idealised soil profile

Soils can be classified into three soil types, dominated by one causal factor. A zonal soil is one whose main characteristics have been determined by climate. An azonal soil is one that is permanently immature (e.g. on steep slopes). An intrazonal soil is one whose main characteristic is determined by parent material (e.g. soils on chalk).

You need to:
- be able to define and understand the origins of soil
- be able to define zonal, azonal and intrazonal soils
- understand the factors that influence soil formation

Soil properties

Soil properties may vary in each horizon and are outlined in the table below.

Soil property	Definition	Importance
Mineral matter	Particles formed as a result of weathering of the parent material	Provides the mineral component of the soil
Soil texture	The size of the particles of mineral matter in the soil — clay, silt, sand, coarse sand (loam is 40% sand, 40% silt and 20% clay)	Controls pore spacing, affecting water and air content and water flow
Organic matter	Material/particles derived from decaying vegetation/animals or faeces; breaks down into humus	Major source of nutrients; holds water; binds soil particles together
Soil structure	The joining together of the mineral and organic particles to form peds — crumb, granular, platy, blocky, prismatic, columnar	Affects water flow, air content and root penetration; influenced by vegetation
Soil moisture	The water held in the soil: gravitational (which drains away and is not available to plants); capillary (available to plant roots); and hygroscopic (unavailable to plants)	The medium by which nutrients are moved in soil (translocation); affects drainage conditions; medium of leaching (minerals in solution) and eluviation (particles in suspension)
Soil air	Fills pore spaces not filled by water; contains more CO_2 and water vapour and less O_2 than air in the atmosphere as a result of bacterial action	Essential for plant growth and respiration of organisms
Soil organisms	Living organisms found in the soil, e.g. bacteria, fungi and earthworms	Decomposition of organic matter (nutrient cycling), nitrogen fixing, development of structure
Soil nutrients	Chemical elements found in the soil which help maintain its fertility	Essential for plant growth; can be translocated (moved) in soil water
Soil acidity	The logarithmic measure of the concentration of hydrogen ions (pH): acid < pH 7; alkaline > pH 7; and neutral — pH 7	Affects plant growth; in UK best is slightly acid; very acid or alkaline inhibits plant growth

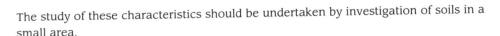

The study of these characteristics should be undertaken by investigation of soils in a small area.

You need to:
- be able to define the main soil characteristics, including texture, structure, acidity and water content
- explain how these characteristics result in different soil horizons
- study soils in a small area to provide examples of these characteristics

Podzols and brown earths

Two of the main zonal (climatic-based) soil types found in the UK are brown earths and podzols. The main characteristics are demonstrated in a diagrammatic comparison of the soil profiles.

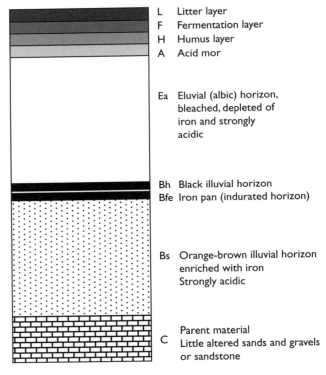

L   Litter layer
F   Fermentation layer
H   Humus layer
A   Acid mor

Ea Eluvial (albic) horizon, bleached, depleted of iron and strongly acidic

Bh Black illuvial horizon
Bfe Iron pan (indurated horizon)

Bs Orange-brown illuvial horizon enriched with iron
Strongly acidic

C   Parent material
Little altered sands and gravels or sandstone

A typical podzol soil profile

Podzols are found under boreal coniferous forest and heathland, especially on sandy, freely drained soils. They have the following characteristics.
- Low temperatures cause low evaporation, but precipitation exceeds evapotranspiration and soil water percolates downwards. Leaching removes soluble minerals and eluviation removes clay and humus particles from the upper horizons (A and E).

- Humic acids from the organic layers (L, F, H, mor) intensify the leaching process (cheluviation).
- A and E horizons consist of bleached, ash-grey sand with a high soil acidity (pH 3–5) because of the lack of clay, humus and nutrients.
- The B horizon has redeposited iron and aluminium, giving an orange-brown colour (Bs). There may be layers of humus particles (Bh) and iron pan (Bfe) where illuviation (deposition) is concentrated.
- Horizons are very clearly defined, because of the processes described above. In addition, the high acidity limits soil fauna and there is no mixing of horizons.

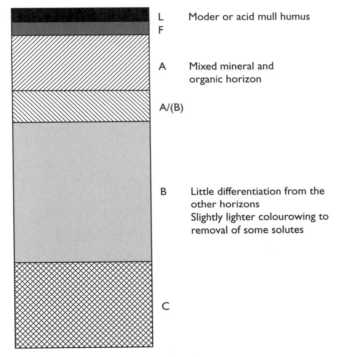

Typical brown earth soil profile

Brown earths are found under temperate deciduous woodland, commonly on clay soils. They are characterised by the following.

- There is a small surplus of precipitation over evapotranspiration, resulting in slight leaching. Soils are consequently mildly acidic (pH 6–6.5). The humus is nutrient-rich (mull) and there are many soil fauna.
- The clays and humus are not removed or redeposited, and the abundant fauna lead to the lack of clear soil horizons.

You need to:

- study the characteristics of two zonal soils, podzols and brown earths   (G)
- understand the conditions that favour the formation of these soils
- be able to compare and contrast the two soil types

The soil catena

This is defined as the changes in soil characteristics down a slope. Catenas develop because the topography causes changes to soil drainage characteristics according to the position and the gradient on the slope. For example, a typical soil catena in the Pennines might comprise: peaty gley podzols on flat, poorly drained summits; podzols on the free-draining slopes; and gley soils on poorly drained slope foot areas.

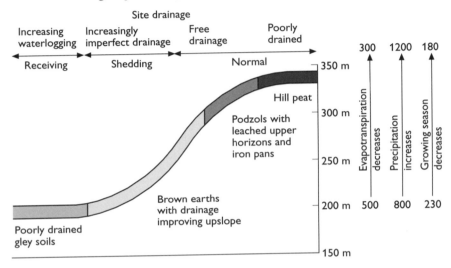

A soil catena in northern England

Human impact on soils: (1) farming

People have a variety of effects on soils. They are able to modify the characteristics of soils to enhance agricultural output, but frequently the effects are unhelpful to the farmer. The main points set out in the specification are shown in the table on page 49.

Organic farming is becoming more popular, in part as a response to the impacts on soil which have arisen from the techniques of modern agriculture. Organic farming involves agricultural techniques that avoid some of the activities and thus the effects outlined in the table above. The use of organic fertilisers maintains soil structure and fertility. The land use is less intensive, thus reducing the need for heavy machinery. Drainage and irrigation may still be necessary but are undertaken sensitively. Crops are rotated to avoid monoculture, and pesticides are organic/biological rather than inorganic.

Compared with conventional farming, organic farming has higher costs. Yields are invariably lower, reducing income per hectare, which is not offset by the higher prices that may be obtained. There are also higher costs associated with conforming to the regulations necessary to ensure produce can be labelled as organic. A small-scale case study would be helpful to demonstrate the costs and benefits of organic farming.

Farming activity	Impact on the soil
Inorganic fertiliser	The nutrients are available in a purer form and are more easily leached as they are freely available. Over a long period of time, the amount of humus in the soil will decrease and the soil structure will be affected. Humus decomposes slowly, the release of nutrients is more gradual, and thus the supply takes place over a longer time scale. Fertility and soil structure are maintained for longer.
Heavy machinery	This affects the soil structure and texture. The soil is compacted and the spaces between the peds and particles reduced. Thus drainage is impaired, causing waterlogging, and the amount of soil air is reduced.
Drainage	This improves the soil for plant growth; it reduces soil moisture and increases soil air. It can involve the construction of sub-surface drains or the break-up of the hardpan frequently found in the B horizon in podzols.
Irrigation	This is carried out to add water to soils. It replaces the soil air. Care is needed to ensure that sufficient water is applied to allow free drainage of water and in warm climates prevent salinisation by capillary action from groundwater.
Monoculture	This is the repeated growing of one crop on the same plot of land. The fertility of the soil is reduced as the same nutrients are taken out. The structure is affected — the humus is not replaced since the vegetation is not replaced after harvesting of the crop.

You need to:

- be aware of the ways in which modern farming methods have affected soils
- consider the impact of inorganic fertilisers, heavy machinery, drainage, irrigation and monoculture
- understand the increasing importance of organic farming for soils
- understand the costs and benefits associated with organic farming in comparison with conventional farming techniques

Human impact on soils: (2) soil degradation

There are three main types of soil degradation: soil erosion, salinisation and desertification. Each involves human failure to manage the soil. The major cause of soil erosion is the removal of vegetation (e.g. rainforest); the major cause of salinisation is poor irrigation procedures (Sudan); and the major cause of desertification is the removal of vegetation in areas of marginal precipitation (Sahel). You need to study one case study to understand the causes (both natural and human), the effects and the conservation measures that are employed.

You need to:

- define and understand the physical and human processes involved in soil erosion, salinisation and desertification

Questions
&
Answers

This section of the guide contains six typical questions for Assessment Unit 1, based on the topic areas outlined in the Content Guidance section.

Please note that in Sections A, B and C, there is only one question offered; in the examination proper there will be two. Section D contains a choice of three questions, but only one should be answered.

Model answers are given after the questions. These are provided at a typical grade-C standard (Candidate A) and a good grade-A standard (Candidate B).

Examiner's comments

The examiner's comments are preceded by the icon ℯ. They are interspersed in the answers and indicate where credit is due. In the weaker answers, they also point out areas for improvement, specific problems and common errors such as poor time management, lack of clarity, weak or non-existent development, irrelevance, mis-interpretation of the question and mistaken meanings of terms.

Marks are awarded according to 'Level' attained. These Levels are allocated marks in the following way:

Sections A, B and C	*Section D*
Level 1: 1–3 marks	Level 1: 1–4 marks
Level 2: 4–5 marks	Level 2: 5–7 marks
Level 3: 6–7 marks	Level 3: 8–10 marks

Water on the land

Question 1

(a) With reference to the hydrological cycle, name two transfers between stores and two outputs. (2 marks)

(b) The diagram below shows a storm hydrograph for an area of pastureland after a rainstorm.

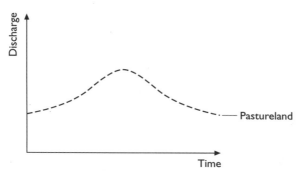

Add to the diagram the likely hydrographs following the same rainstorm in areas of similar physical conditions for:

(i) an area of dense woodland

(ii) an urbanised area (2 marks)

(c) Explain the differences in the shapes of the hydrographs shown in (b). (4 marks)

(d) Why is flooding an increasing hazard in the UK? (7 marks)

■ ■ ■

Answer to question 1: Candidate A

(a) Transfers: infiltration and interception
Outputs: precipitation and transpiration

> ℮ This response shows some confusion. One of the transfers named (interception) and one of the outputs (precipitation) are incorrect, so 1 mark is lost.

(b)

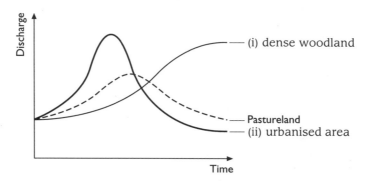

🖉 Candidate A has identified the urban hydrograph correctly, but shows confusion over the woodland one, losing 1 mark. This is another factual question — the diagrams will be either right or wrong. The key is to identify that the pasture hydrograph will be between the urban and the woodland hydrographs.

(c) The urban hydrograph has a steep rising limb and more gentle recession limb. The lag time is short. This is because the urban area has few trees to intercept and the land surface is tarmac. Water cannot infiltrate and runs off to the rivers quickly in the drains. The woodland hydrograph has a very long lag time and this is because the trees intercept a lot of the water. More water can soak into the ground and it reaches the river slowly. The water eventually reaches the river and the discharge increases rapidly and is very great.

🖉 The response does try to explain the hydrographs. The urban explanation is mostly correct, with some geographical language. The confusion over the woodland explanation is reflected in the inaccuracy seen in part (b), but some elements are correct. However, the use of English and geographical terminology is less secure than would be expected in a grade A response. This answer gains 2 out of the 4 marks available.

(d) Flooding is quite common in the UK. Flooding occurs for a number of reasons. Deforestation causes flooding. The removal of the trees means that there is less interception and infiltration, and overland flow occurs. As more land is used for farming, more surface runoff takes place. Urban areas now cover more of the UK and this means that the land surface does not allow water to infiltrate. The water reaches the rivers in drains more quickly. People now build on floodplains as demand for housing increases and when rivers flood, they are exposed to the hazard. Many rivers flood naturally in spring when snows melt. Rivers are flooding more as shown by the floods in York.

🖉 This response lacks confidence. There is an awareness of the increasing hazard, but it is not consistently covered. The simple reference to the example comes at the end, but the theoretical points are valid. Language is less competent and the structure does not have paragraphs, a clear introduction or a conclusion. As mentioned in the introduction (p. 7), part (d) would be marked according to Levels, this one reaching Level 2, with 4 marks.

■ ■ ■

Answer to question 1: Candidate B

(a) Transfers: infiltration and throughflow
Outputs: evaporation and transpiration

🖉 This question uses a straightforward command word which requires straightforward responses. In this case, one word will suffice for each, and all four stated are correct, for full marks.

(b)

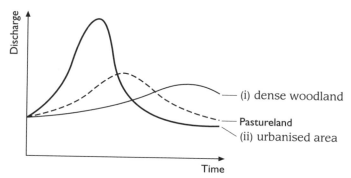

(i) dense woodland

Pastureland

(ii) urbanised area

Time

e Candidate B correctly identifies the differences between the hydrographs. The urban hydrograph is very steep and declines rapidly. The woodland hydrograph is lower than the pasture one. Full marks are awarded here.

(c) The urban hydrograph rises steeply and declines slightly more gently, with a very short lag time. This is because there is little vegetation to allow interception and infiltration. The urban land surface is impermeable and water runs off rapidly into the drains and reaches the river very quickly. On the other hand, the woodland hydrograph has a gentle rising limb and an even more gentle recession limb. This is because the dense vegetation intercepts most of the precipitation, causes it to reach the ground gradually and to be infiltrated. More water will reach the river as groundwater flow, with very little overland flow. Hence the long lag time.

e The command word here is important. This response does explain the differences in the shapes of the hydrographs and there is good use of appropriate geographical vocabulary and language. This is a wordy answer and some of the descriptive points might have been left out, but full marks are awarded for the explanation offered.

(d) Flooding is an increasing hazard in the UK as shown by the recent flooding around York.

Flooding occurs around York for natural reasons. It is the confluence of tributaries of the River Ouse, and after a long period of rain over the Pennines the waters reach York at the same time, and the river floods. Flooding is increased if snow melt occurs or rain falls onto an already saturated surface; overland flow will be dominant.

Human influences have increased the frequency of flooding. The draining of peat on the uplands has increased water flow, and the Vale of York is arable land allowing much overland flow. Also, the increase in settlement in the Ouse basin has increased the impermeability of the land surface and water reaches the rivers more quickly via the efficient drains. More development occurs on river floodplains meaning that more property is affected by flooding.

In conclusion, a combination of physical and human factors has increased the hazard of flooding in the UK in recent years.

e The command word requires explanation, but the key words are *increasing* and *hazard*. Simple explanations of flooding will not be totally relevant: there must be reasons for the changing occurrence. This response covers both human and physical factors applied to a case study. The factors are correctly identified, and explanation is offered. There is good use of geographical terminology and there is a clear structure to the response, with an introduction, paragraphs and a conclusion. The response covers both the *increasing* and the *hazard* elements, and attains the top of Level 3, for 7 marks.

Climatic hazards and change

Question 2

Study the table below which shows average precipitation (mm) for typical stations in tropical monsoon (TM) and cool temperate western maritime (CTWM) climates.

	Jan	Feb	Mar	Apr	May	Jun	Jul	Aug	Sep	Oct	Nov	Dec	Total
Bombay TM	0	0	0	0	20	480	620	340	265	65	10	0	1800
Paris CTWM	60	50	35	40	60	55	60	65	55	50	50	50	630

(a) Compare and contrast the annual pattern of precipitation for these two types of climate. (4 marks)

(b) For one of these climatic types, give reasons for the annual pattern of precipitation.* (4 marks)

(c) Outline the costs and benefits for human activity in areas with the tropical monsoon type of climate. (7 marks)

(*Each candidate has provided two answers to part (b), one for each climatic type. This is simply for the benefit of the reader.)

■ ■ ■

Answer to question 2: Candidate A

(a) It is clear that the TM climate has a seasonal rainfall pattern, with the rain falling in summer, but not in winter (December to April). The peak is in July when over 600 mm occurs. In the CTWM climate, rain occurs in every month, with March the lowest (35 mm) and August the highest (65 mm).

🖉 This is an accurate response for 2 marks. Both climates are covered, and there is reference to the data, though not consistently. However, there is no accommodation of the command words so this loses half of the available marks, regardless of the quality of the response.

(b) In the TM climate the seasonal pattern of precipitation is caused by the movement of the ITCZ. In winter it has moved southwards and cold Siberian air blows over Bombay. This is dry air so no rain occurs. In summer the ITCZ moves back and brings the rain as the low-pressure belt moves northwards. This is wet air as it has passed over the sea.

🖉 This response is generally correct, though the odd slip occurs (the Siberian air mass is not cold by the time it reaches Bombay). There is a lack of detail and precision, though the use of language is generally correct. The points made have some support, but they are not developed fully to provide detailed explanation. For example, the transitional periods are not covered. Only 2 marks are awarded.

(b) In the CTWM climate the even monthly amounts of rainfall (35–65 mm) are the result of the depressions which affect this part of the world. These occur all year. The depressions form over the Atlantic, and frontal rain falls at warm and cold fronts as they pass over this part of Europe. In summer there is more convectional rain as thunderstorms occur.

> ✒ This is a very generalised, yet basically correct response for 2 marks. There is a clear understanding, but points are not fully developed. There are references to the data, but these are not consistently made. The response identifies the convectional rainfall in summer, but the explanation is not developed.

(c) The monsoon rains are essential for farming in this area and crops such as rice are planted for the start of the rains. Flooding is essential for the rice to grow, and water is stored to make a longer growing season. Wheat is grown in areas where the precipitation is lower in the north of India. The heavy rains have caused flooding in parts of India. Soil erosion and damage to roads and settlements have occurred when rains are very heavy, e.g. Bangladesh and Nepal. Tourism is also affected by the rains, so it tends to be more developed in the dry season.

> ✒ This is a brief response, but a number of valid costs and benefits are mentioned. Support is not consistent and few specific locations are offered. Two factors are covered, so an understanding of the topic is demonstrated. However, points are not well developed. This is at the lower end of Level 2, and gains 4 marks.

■ ■ ■

Answer to question 2: Candidate B

(a) The TM climate has a very clear seasonal distribution of precipitation. No precipitation falls between December and April inclusive, the great majority of it occurring in June to September, reaching a peak of 620 mm in July. On the other hand, precipitation is more evenly spread in the CTWM climate, with precipitation occurring in all months of the year, with a range of 35 mm in March to 65 mm in August. This gives a slight summer maximum, as in the TM area, but January, the wettest winter month, does have 60 mm.

> ✒ This response covers both climates and does have clear elements of comparison and contrast, so full marks. The table of data is used effectively to make the points.

(b) In the TM climate the pattern of precipitation is a result of the movement of the ITCZ. The ITCZ is an area of low pressure at the meeting of the NE and SE trades, where maximum solar radiation causes a belt of heavy precipitation to occur. The ITCZ moves south in the winter (December–March) and high pressure over Siberia causes dry winds to blow out over Bombay. In summer (June–September) the ITCZ moves northwards as low pressure forms over Siberia, drawing in the moist tropical air from over the Indian Ocean to produce the heavy precipitation. The precipitation is lower as the ITCZ advances and retreats (May, September, October).

✍ This is a complete response, for full marks. The explanation is present, covering pressure changes, air mass variations and global circulation patterns. Reference is made to location and the seasonal element is well focused. There is also mention of the transition as the monsoon rains advance and retreat, including definition of the seasons.

(b) The CTWM climate is strongly influenced by the low pressure systems of the westerly wind belt. The precipitation is evenly spread as the depressions formed at the meeting of polar and tropical maritime air masses cause precipitation by frontal uplift. These are more frequent in winter when Paris would be in the track of the depressions, but they can occur all year, hence the limited monthly range from 35 to 65 mm. In summer, high-pressure systems are more frequent, but the maximum of 65 mm for August is a result of intense heating, causing convectional thunderstorms.

✍ This response follows the command word and provides reasons, and gains full marks. The pressure systems for summer and winter are covered and frontal precipitation identified as a major contributor. The identification of the influence of convectional precipitation in summer is the mark of a very good response.

(c) The TM climate has many benefits for human activity.

The farming system is adapted to the seasonal pattern of rainfall, and crops (e.g. rice) are planted to coincide with the arrival of the monsoon. Flooding itself is a natural process, which provides silt for the floodplain fields. The dry season has caused water management so that storage of the rains and irrigation can extend the growing season and the number of crops harvested each year (e.g. rice in Bali). The failure or delay of the monsoon rains has a devastating effect on farming, causing famine (e.g. NW India). Tourism is influenced by the climate. The best time to visit is in the dry season when poor weather is unlikely (e.g. Goa or Taj Mahal). In the rainy season poor weather hinders visibility and travel. In late summer and autumn the Bay of Bengal is subject to cyclones which cause much economic dislocation to Bangladesh. In the late summer of 2000, landslides affected Assam when intense, above average precipitation was experienced.

Therefore, there are both costs and benefits for people arising from the TM climate.

✍ This is a well argued response. The use of support comes from a number of brief references, rather than a more detailed case study, but it is consistent. Both costs and benefits are covered, and farming, tourism and general economic development are mentioned. There is a brief introduction and conclusion.

Energy and life

Question 3

(a) Distinguish between the *biotic* and *abiotic* elements of an ecosystem. (2 marks)

(b) Study the energy pyramid below.

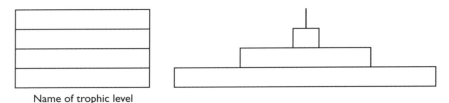

Name of trophic level

    (i) Name the trophic levels in the boxes provided. (2 marks)

    (ii) Why is so little energy passed on from one trophic level to the next? (4 marks)

(c) With reference to *one* biome, examine the factors which account for its natural productivity. (7 marks)

■ ■ ■

Answer to question 3: Candidate A

(a) The biotic element is the living parts of the ecosystem such as plants and animals. The abiotic element is the non-living element.

    e One basic distinction is provided, for 1 mark. The definitions are accurate, but there is a lack of examples to qualify the statements.

(b) (i) Grass, mouse, snake, bird.

    e This demonstrates the principles, by using examples, but does not use the correct names of the trophic levels and therefore gains no marks.

(b) (ii) The transfer of energy between trophic levels is inefficient because it is lost in the transfer. Energy is lost in breathing, living, decay and excretion. Meat eaters are inefficient users of energy in that, compared with the energy available as plants, only 1% of energy is used by the meat eaters.

    e This response shows some understanding of the reasons, which are offered in a rather simplistic way. Some credit (2 marks) can be awarded. However, there is digression away from the theme into the consequences of this energy loss, which was not requested.

(c) The tropical rainforest biome is the most productive biome. The solar radiation is at its greatest all year and temperatures are high all of the time. The rainfall is high and there is no dry season, so that plants can grow all year round. This means that productivity is very great and there is much organic matter as the biomass, which is the weight of matter per metre squared. Thus there are many factors affecting productivity.

📝 This response shows an understanding of the main concepts. Although there is no specific definition as an introduction, one is given later. There is a simple introduction and a conclusion; a number of valid factors are covered, but there is not the detailed knowledge or geographical terminology needed to gain high marks. This response reaches the top of Level 2, for 5 marks.

■ ■ ■

Answer to question 3: Candidate B

(a) The abiotic element is the non-living component of the ecosystem, e.g. soil, water and air. In contrast, the biotic element is the living element, e.g. fauna and flora.

📝 This is a straightforward, accurate definition with a clear distinction, for full marks.

(b) (i) Producer, primary consumer, secondary consumer, tertiary consumer.

📝 This is correct. Alternatively, any correct combination of plants, herbivores, carnivores, omnivores, or an acceptable alternative would gain full marks.

(b) (ii) Energy is created by solar radiation converted into organic matter by photosynthesis. At each trophic level energy is lost by respiration, excretion, decomposition and heat which are lost between transfer to the next level, resulting in only 10% of energy being passed on. For example, when we eat meat only 10% is converted into organic matter as the actions of breathing, excretion and living cause energy to be lost, i.e. we are unable to convert all of the material into energy.

📝 This is a very good response. The reasons for energy loss are here, meeting the demands of the command word, and these are exemplified. Full marks are awarded. A diagram could be helpful here and would gain appropriate credit.

(c) The example of a biome is tropical rainforest. This is the most productive biome on earth.

Net primary productivity is defined as the mass (g/m^2pa) of organic matter produced after losses by respiration etc. and can be expressed thus: net primary productivity = $P - R$, where P = productivity and R = respiration.

The rainforest has ideal conditions for plant growth, with high annual temperatures (over 25°C) all year, so there is an all-year growing season. The greatest amount of solar radiation is received here, as the sun is high in the sky all year. In addition, precipitation is heavy (over 2000 mm pa) and occurs all year, and there is a water surplus available for plant growth.

Therefore, a range of factors is responsible for the productivity of this biome.

📝 This is a very full response at the top of Level 3, for full marks. A range of factors is covered and examined, as required by the command word. The named biome is appropriate and there is a clear definition, thus setting the scene. The introduction, development of the points and the conclusion indicate a grade-A answer. There are no specific examples quoted in this response, but the level of understanding is very good. Reference might have been made to the rate of decomposition of organic matter to maintain the nutrient cycle, so that nutrient losses are minimised.

ection

D

Extended prose

Answer one question from this section.

Question 4

(a) Outline the reasons for the management of river basins.   (10 marks)

(b) Examine the costs and benefits of *one* example of river basin management.   (10 marks)

Question 5

(a) Outline the ways in which urban areas may influence weather and climate.   (10 marks)

(b) How successful have been the strategies used to improve urban air quality in a
    city you have studied?   (10 marks)

Question 6

(a) In what ways and why are brown earths and podzols different?   (10 marks)

(b) Explain how modern farming methods can modify these soil types.   (10 marks)

■ ■ ■

Answer to question 4: Candidate A

(a) River basins are managed for many reasons, usually to prevent flooding having a damaging impact on people. Rivers tend to flood every year when heavy rainfall or snow melt occurs and as more people live on floodplains or near rivers, more are affected by this flooding.

   The control of flooding is the main reason for the management of rivers, as seen recently in the case of the Mississippi. Here the amount of water was totally unexpected for the time of year. The heavy rainfall meant that the river levels rose and overflowed, causing billions of dollars worth of damage. So, as a response, more effort has been put in to make sure that this does not happen again.

   Rivers are also controlled to use the river for the benefit of people. For example, locks have been built on the Rhine to enable better navigation, as well as flood control. In addition, the Rhine has been harnessed for HEP, which supplies both homes and industry.

   Rivers are also managed to make sure that flooding is not caused by changes in land use, such as urbanisation. The building of settlements near the river causes more water to reach the river quickly, as less infiltration occurs.

   e This response shows a fair degree of understanding. There are examples, though these are not provided consistently. The style is good, with an introduction and development of points in paragraphs, but there is no conclusion. Some good geographical language is used, but not all points are fully explained and there is a drift into river management, rather than a focus on the basin. This is a clear Level 2 response, gaining 6 marks.

(b) The River Colorado is a good example of river management. It has had many dams built on it, originally to prevent flooding, but since the Second World War other factors have been important and these have had many benefits and costs.

　　The main benefits are flood control; the river has not flooded since 1935, apart from one time in 1993. The flood control is so effective that the river does not reach the sea in Mexico any more, causing problems for Mexican farmers. Also, the dams produce a lot of HEP for industry and settlement in California.

　　Water is also used for irrigation in California, Arizona and Utah, but is saltier than many rivers and has to be used carefully, otherwise salinisation can occur.

　　Tourism is now important, and many visitors come to use the lakes and enjoy the scenery in the National Parks, such as the Grand Canyon. This causes pollution as tourists always leave litter.

　　In conclusion, there are many benefits and costs in this river management scheme, but the advantages are more important.

> 🖉 This response does show understanding. A number of points are correctly made but they are not all fully developed and support is not consistent. There is some imbalance in that benefits are clearly stated, but the costs are under-emphasised and seem to be included as an afterthought. There is an introduction, a conclusion and some development of the theme, giving this response a Level 2 mark of 6.

■ ■ ■

Answer to question 4: Candidate B

(a) River basins are managed for several reasons. These include the control of the river basin to prevent damage to people and property, and control of the river basin to improve the river for human activities.

　　The main reason to prevent damage is the need to control flooding. Most rivers flood naturally due to periodic variations in river flow, which result in the river overflowing its banks and inundating the floodplain. This causes much damage to property and disruption to economic activity, as shown by the Mississippi floods of 1993 when total damage was over $10.5 billion, there were 45 deaths and over 45 000 people were evacuated.

　　River basins are also managed to improve the river for people. The building of dams as part of a river management scheme will not only provide flood control in the first instance, but will store water for industrial, agricultural and domestic use — particularly useful in areas of potential water shortage. Dam construction may also improve the river for navigation and tourist activities, for example, as well as providing cheap HEP. This can be seen in the management of the River Colorado, USA, which will be developed as the case in part (b).

　　The management of river basins is essential to minimise the effects of land-use changes in the basin. For example, the clearing of vegetation on a large scale is likely to cause severe soil erosion and slope failure on a large scale and add to flooding levels downstream as silt is eroded and builds up in river channels. The increased overland flow resulting from deforestation will further add to the flood risk in the basin, as seen in Nepal and Bangladesh in recent years. Reafforestation is undertaken to reduce these risks and thus manage the basin on a larger scale.

In conclusion, there are a number of reasons for the management of river basins, either to prevent harm or to use them for the benefit of people.

e This response covers a number of valid reasons, as required by the command words, and gains full marks. There is an introduction to set the scene and classify these reasons. The points are wide-ranging and are developed by paragraphs, with specific support and a conclusion. There is understanding, a range of supported points, and a well-written argument, using specialist vocabulary.

(b) I shall use the River Colorado to answer this section. This is a well-established river basin management scheme. There are both costs and benefits, which will be discussed in my answer.

There are probably more benefits arising from the management of the scheme, otherwise it would not have been undertaken. The main benefits include flood control, the generation of HEP, the development of farming through irrigation, the provision of water for urban areas and the opportunities for recreation which have arisen.

The construction of the dams, starting with the Hoover Dam in 1935, has meant that flooding has almost ceased (there were floods in the Parker Valley in 1993). This has caused the cost of the lack of sediment reaching the mouth of the river which was a valuable source of alluvium. In addition, the dams will eventually silt up. The Colorado no longer flows into the sea, causing agriculture to decline and the delta to become a saline wasteland.

The dams are also major sources of HEP, providing a much-needed energy source to the southwest of the country. Water for irrigation now supplies farmers in Wyoming, Utah, Arizona and California. The water is cheap and plentiful, but is not used efficiently and is relatively saline, so care has to be taken in its use. California has the largest urban areas supplied, and conservation measures are in place for when drought occurs.

Recreation has expanded in recent years as the population of the southwest USA has increased. Tourism is a major sector of the economy, with over 1.5 million visitors each year. The popularity of this area has meant that further dam schemes have been opposed on environmental grounds in National Parks.

Overall, the benefits covered above outweigh the costs, but the negative impacts are great in localised areas. The USA benefits mostly, with Mexico facing the greater costs.

e This is another well-written response, for full marks. There is detailed under-standing of the topic, with consistent support. The command words are followed, in that costs and benefits are examined, and there is use of appropriate language. There is a clear introduction and a conclusion, and paragraphs are used.

■ ■ ■

Answer to question 5: Candidate A

(a) There are many ways in which towns and cities affect climate and weather. In general, the bigger the town, the more effects there are.

The urban heat island is a very important effect. The buildings absorb heat from the sun in the day and release it at night. Heat from central heating, traffic, industry and people is also released. This has the effect of raising temperatures in urban areas, on a daily and even an annual basis. On a daily basis, night-time temperatures are raised by about 3°C (London) but the effect is much less during the day. The temperatures are higher in comparison with the surrounding rural areas. Annual temperatures are also higher, by about 1°C in London.

Wind speeds are reduced in urban areas, because of the building heights causing more friction. However, very high buildings produce very high wind speeds because the winds are forced between them like canyons, often strong enough to blow people over.

There is less snow in towns due to the higher temperatures, and more cloud and rainfall as the higher temperatures cause more convection. There is less sunlight because of the greater amount of particles in the air.

Therefore, there are a number of ways in which towns affect climate and weather.

> There is a range of points covered here, showing understanding, but there are some omissions, for example the role of anticyclones and detail on the points covered. The content is accurate, but examples are used inconsistently. In addition, points are not fully developed. There is a brief introduction and conclusion. The use of geographical language is relevant and the use of English is competent. This reaches Level 2 and gains 7 marks.

(b) Air quality in towns and cities has changed greatly in recent years. I have studied Athens as a case study. Car pollution has become one of the major sources of air pollution in cities, though the gases are also emitted by industry.

The gases that come out of the exhausts include carbon monoxide, carbon dioxide, nitrogen oxides and hydrocarbons and are increasing as more cars are on the roads. These build up and react with sunlight to form chemical smog in high-pressure weather conditions.

The Greek authorities have introduced several measures. They have introduced a scheme to only allow certain cars into Athens on certain days. This was done by the use of odd and even number plates on alternate days. People got round this by having two cars with different numbered plates, so it wasn't very successful. Catalytic converters are now compulsory for new cars under EU legislation, but there are many old cars still in use. Diesel cars are supposed to be less polluting, but they emit particles that cause breathing problems, thus adding to health problems.

Therefore, attempts to improve air quality have been only partially successful, mainly because people want to drive cars for convenience.

🖉 There is a clear essay format, with an introduction and conclusion. The theme is kept in mind, with reference to a case study, but detail on the strategies is limited. Three strategies are mentioned and there is some simple evaluation of the success. There are some slips; carbon dioxide is not a polluting gas in this context, for example. There is some good knowledge demonstrated on the range of strategies, and the reference to values and attitudes is worthy of credit. Overall, this is a good level 2 response, gaining 7 marks.

■ ■ ■

Answer to question 5: Candidate B

(a) Urban areas have a strong influence on weather and climate; the actual impact is greater the larger the urban area. There are a number of impacts, including temperature, winds, relative humidity, air quality, cloud, precipitation and sunlight.

One of the earliest studies was of London. Research showed that temperature was greatly modified. The buildings absorb solar radiation in the day and release it at night, along with the heat generated by industry, vehicles, people and the heating of the buildings themselves. The effect is known as the urban heat island. This shows that, on average, temperatures are 0.6°C warmer in the day and 3°C to 4°C warmer at night when compared with the surrounding rural areas. The night-time temperature differences are greatest under anticyclonic conditions when there are only very gentle winds, if any. Climate is also affected, as mean annual temperatures are 1.3°C warmer in London than the surrounding area. Relative humidity tends to be lower because of the higher temperatures and the lack of transpiration from vegetation.

The friction of the buildings reduces wind velocities by up to 30%, but there is increased turbulence. High-rise buildings channel winds to very high velocities.

Precipitation is increased over urban areas by about 10% because of more intense convection producing a greater number of thunderstorms. Cloud is increased for the same reasons. Snow is less frequent because of the higher temperatures.

The incidence of fog is greater because of the greater concentration of particles, though higher temperatures counterbalance this. There is less sunlight because of these particles, which can reflect up to 50% of radiation when the sun is low in the sky.

In recent years there has been an increase in pollution from motor vehicles, especially sulphur dioxide, nitrogen oxides, carbon monoxide and hydrocarbons. Under anticyclonic conditions, especially in summer, photochemical smog is formed which reduces solar radiation and visibility.

These are some of the influences that urban areas have on climate and weather.

🖉 This is an inclusive response. A good range of points is covered and discussed, meeting the demands of the command words. Detailed understanding is demonstrated, with examples. There is an introduction, development of the points and a conclusion, albeit brief. The use of geographical language is very good, as is the use of English. This is a top Level 3 response, for 10 marks.

(b) Urban air quality has been of increasing importance in recent years, and legislation has been enforced with the aim of improving the situation.

The rise of the internal combustion engine has brought new sources of pollution to urban areas. The unburned gases from exhausts have increased in concentration. These include sulphur dioxide, nitrogen oxides, carbon monoxide and hydrocarbons. These are now found in such concentrations, especially in anti-cyclonic conditions, when a chemical reaction with sunlight forms photochemical smog, that they are a real hazard to those with respiratory problems.

In Los Angeles, the pollution has been increased by the morphology of the land as the city is in a basin and polluting air cannot escape so easily. The city author-ities have been in the forefront in efforts to reduce the impact of this pollution.

A range of strategies has been established. Strategies having a direct impact include the use of catalytic converters, which have been mandatory for many years, the insistence on 'lean burn' engines and research into new fuels, including hydrogen and electric powered cars and buses. These have had a beneficial impact, though the latter are not yet fully operational and there are more cars on the roads. The Los Angeles authorities have recently announced that the last freeway is being constructed. This may reduce vehicle movements in the future.

Other strategies have focused on changing peoples' behaviour. Car sharing has been encouraged by the use of priority traffic lanes reserved for cars that have more than one person in. This has been very succesful in cutting journey times for those involved. All businesses have to have in place a policy to reduce the number of car journeys made by their employees, and there are favourable tax incentives for such businesses.

However, the attachment of the American driver to the car is well documented and the success of such strategies in Los Angeles will always be in doubt. Some are more effective than others, but the range of policies will need to be in place for the full picture to be seen. This will not be until 2010 at the earliest.

> *e* This is a very good response, for full marks. There is good understanding shown, and the subject knowledge is well developed. There are other pollutants that could have been included, but the quality of the response confirms a high mark. Examples are presented consistently. There is an introduction and conclusion, with development of the points. The command word is important in such a question and the response is careful to include evaluation, as requested.

■ ■ ■

Answer to question 6: Candidate A

(a) Podzols and brown earths are found in different parts of the world. Podzols are found under coniferous forest on sandy soils and brown earths under deciduous woodland.

The cold conditions mean that pine needles do not break down very easily and this makes the podzols very acidic. Snow melt in spring percolates down through the layer of litter, and leaches the minerals from the upper horizons. The A1 is stained black with humus and the A2 is ash grey as the humus is leached out. The iron and clay are also leached from these horizons. The B horizon has a hard pan of iron at the top, with a layer of redeposited humus, but the rest of it is orange/brown and clayey as the minerals and particles are deposited.

The brown earth is not strongly leached. The plant litter is mull and it breaks down easily. There is a layer of humus and the A1 horizon is brown with humus. The A2 is leached so is a lighter brown. The B is red/brown as the iron is deposited. These do not form on sandy soils, but more frequently on clays.

Thus the soils are different because they have different rates of leaching, plant litter and parent material.

e This response shows some understanding of the main concepts. There is an introduction and a conclusion, with both soil types covered. The use of geographical vocabulary is good. The main weakness of this response is the failure to contrast the two directly so that the differences are implicit rather than explicit. This response reaches Level 2 and gains 6 marks.

(b) Modern farming methods can modify these soils in many ways.

The podzol has to be modified the most, as it is not a naturally fertile soil. As it is so acidic it has to have fertilisers added to make it suitable for crops. Lime is the most common. Organic fertilisers are helpful to increase the water content of the soil. Clay can also be added to make the texture better for farming. If there is a hardpan, the podzol will be waterlogged and this will need to be removed to allow drainage. Crops will be grown which will be able to change the humus content and make it less acidic.

If the podzol is farmed then heavy machinery may cause compaction of the soil, affecting structure and drainage. Soil erosion may occur when the soil has been ploughed and left exposed to the weather.

Brown earths do not need much modification, as they are good for farming. They are naturally fertile.

Modern farming methods can modify both these soil types, one needing to be modified more than the other.

e This shows understanding, especially of the podzol. However, the use of geographical language is weak and the English simplistic. There is an introduction and a conclusion. The main limitation is that the response is unbalanced, covering more on the podzol than the brown earth. It is this imbalance that loses marks and puts this response at Level 2, for 5 marks.

■ ■ ■

Answer to question 6: Candidate B

(a) Brown earths and podzols are two zonal soils, that is, they are soils strongly influenced by climate and vegetation and occur over large areas of the world. Podzols are typically found under coniferous (boreal) forest, whereas brown earths are found under temperate deciduous woodland. This is a generalisation in that local relief, geology and drainage conditions also have a strong influence at a local scale.

Podzols are best-developed on well-drained parent materials, especially sand. This allows water to percolate freely in summer and strong leaching to occur. The pine needles, having waxy cuticles, are slow to decompose and the freezing conditions in winter inhibit the decomposers. The litter ferments, increasing the acidity of the percolating water and increasing the leaching of nutrients. Most leaching occurs as the snows melt in spring. The A1 horizon is stained black with mor humus, but the leaching of iron sesquioxides and eluviation of particles causes the A2 or E horizon to be ash grey in colour and sandy in texture. The upper B horizon frequently has a layer of redeposited iron pan (which can produce water-logging), a layer of redeposited humus, and below this is the orange/brown B horizon, with colouring the result of the redeposition of iron. It has a very clayey texture caused by the illuviation of the clay particles.

In contrast, the brown earth's horizons are less well defined. The litter is less acidic and is decomposed more quickly — thus the percolating water is less acidic. There is no layer of fermenting litter, but one of mull humus. Thus, leaching is less strong as the parent material is not sand but loam. In addition, there is sufficient percolation of water to cause leaching, but not podzolisation, and the horizons are less clearly distinguishable. The A1 horizon is dark brown as the earthworms mix in the humus, rather than black, so there is less humus staining and the A2 horizon is a lighter brown as a result of leaching of iron. The B horizon is more red/brown as the iron is redeposited. There is no hardpan and clay is found in all horizons, so brown earths are more fertile than podzols.

Thus the differences between the two soils are the result of variations in the amount and rate of downward percolating water, the type of humus, the rate of decomposition and the parent material.

> *e* Very good understanding is clearly shown in this response, which gains full marks. There is excellent use of geographical language and detail is clearly presented. The command words are followed and the differences are clearly contrasted. There is a competent introduction and a conclusion.

(b) Modern farming methods have, in many ways, a stronger impact on podzols as they are more difficult to use for farming. Brown earths, on the other hand, are suitable for farming without great modification.

Brown earths are naturally suitable for farming. They are slightly acidic, with a good texture and structure, though they may require the addition of lime. Once the woodland has been cleared, ploughing is used and the soil makes good arable land. They are humus rich, with plentiful soil fauna. Once used, the brown earths do have to be maintained, and the application of fertilisers is necessary. Poor management will lead to soil erosion, so the structure of the soil should be maintained by the use of organic fertilisers.

On the other hand, podzols are a challenge to the farmer. The high acidity has to be tackled by liming. The free drainage of the sands is changed by the application of clay and organic fertilisers to improve water retention, reduce leaching and improve the soil structure. The hard pan will need to be either ploughed or destroyed in other ways to ensure the drainage of the soil. The removal of the conifers or heath vegetation and its replacement with crops or livestock will change the type of litter and increase the soil fauna. This is an expensive process, and the farmer must be confident of suitable returns before commencing.

In conclusion, modern farming methods can modify both of these soil types, one more strongly than the other. Both will require care to ensure fertility is retained.

✓ This shows a great deal of understanding. Although there are alternative approaches to this topic, for example covering the damage caused to brown earths by compaction, ploughing and soil erosion, this is a valid response. The use of geographical and English vocabulary is accurate and shows attention to detail. Note that the use of examples in this case is by type of modification, rather than by location. There is an introduction, good coverage of both soil types, and a conclusion. Thus is another Level 3 answer, but at the lower end of the band (8 marks) because of the lack of specific examples.